Editorial
Another Europe Is Possible
Our Common Security

The North Atlantic Treaty Organisation meets in Warsaw in July 2016. Amid much talk of 'Russian aggression', the Alliance will set out plans to deploy a 'Russia-deterrent force in the Baltic and Black Sea regions', according to *EU Observer*, while Montenegro's application for membership will be approved.

The United States has already announced substantial increases in military expenditure in Europe to counter the 'Russian threat', while the Rand Corporation declares that the Baltic states of Estonia, Latvia and Lithuania could be overrun in a matter of hours. President Putin remarks that Russia already has enough land (now including Crimea) and doesn't want more. Meanwhile, Russia steps up its own military preparedness and expenditure, and is particularly sensitive about US military manouevres close to Kaliningrad, the Russian enclave on the Baltic Sea.

How is Europe's common security to be safeguarded in this fraught and deepening confrontation? In the Sixteenth Century, Ivan IV (the 'Terrible') of Russia sought an alliance with England against Poland and Lithuania. Queen Elizabeth I had sent traders by sea to Muscovy where, it seems, they were courteously received. Russia would trade furs, timber and gold for military kit and artisans skilled in producing it. The pattern is a familiar one, and the significance of NATO's choice of Warsaw for its 2016 Summit will not have been lost on Russia nor, for contrasting reasons, on neighbouring countries, many of which are former members of the Warsaw Pact. The Polish defence minister recently asserted that 'all Russian behaviour attests to systematic preparation for aggressive action'. Meanwhile, war in Ukraine flares again, while further away in the southern Caucasus conflicts in Azerbaijan and Georgia go unresolved.

In the United Kingdom, there is a referendum on membership of the European Union, but not on that of NATO, the nuclear armed treaty organisation. In this issue of *The Spokesman*, Stuart Holland addresses democratic alternatives for a Europe prepared to go beyond austerity, while reminding us how European Nuclear Disarmament helped reverse the trend towards 'theatre nuclear war' in the 1980s. END, as it was known, helped to bring about the landmark Intermediate Nuclear Forces Treaty, which outlaws a whole class of nuclear weapons. Perhaps with these precedents in mind, the International Peace Bureau convenes a World

Congress in Berlin at the end of September with the aim of creating an action agenda 'For a Climate of Peace'. Europe and the wider world are much in need of such initiatives.

* * *

Germany's influential role in Eurasian developments underpinned events earlier in 2016. 'Berlin wasn't chosen by chance,' Yanis Varoufakis told *The Spokesman* at the launch of DiEM25 (short for Democracy in Europe Movement 2025) in February 2016. Of course, Germany is the dominant force in the European Union. In 2017, Germany has a general election as well as heading the G20 group of major economies. So, if you seek to build a political movement at the European level, as Mr Varoufakis avows, there are compelling reasons to announce it in Germany's thriving capital city.

Certainly, participation at DiEM's initial gathering was drawn from many of the European Union's 28 countries, including significant representation from the eastern '11' stretching from the Baltics into the Balkans, as well as core Europe (France, Germany, Belgium), southern Europe (Greece, of course, Italy, Portugal, Spain) including recently elected municipal representatives of 'rebel cities' such as Barcelona and Madrid, and vocal input from Ireland and, to a lesser extent, from the United Kingdom.

A generation or so earlier, in 1983, the European Nuclear Disarmament (END) Convention met in divided Berlin's vast International Congress Centre. This was a key moment in the mass campaign against the increasing threat of 'limited' nuclear war in Europe. The United States was deploying nuclear-armed cruise missiles on the territories of five western European members of NATO, including West Germany, which was also to host the super-fast Pershing II missiles. These latter weapons could strike targets in the Soviet Union in a matter of minutes. For its part, the USSR deployed mobile SS20 nuclear-armed missiles and other nuclear-armed munitions which could hit targets in western Europe. Germany was very much in the firing line, and the widespread unease this created, including in the military, is rather well captured in 'Deutschland 83', the hit, pro-NATO television drama.

Rather more significantly, the END Convention in Berlin raised the question of German reunification, much to the chagrin of the Soviet Peace Committee, which publicly denounced the Bertrand Russell Peace Foundation and the END Conventions it helped organise. Six years later, in 1989, the Berlin Wall came down in the first of a series of 'velvet revolutions' across the countries of the soon-to-be-dissolved Warsaw Pact.

Berlin felt first hand the effect of these fundamental changes in European geopolitics.

Nowadays, Mr Varoufakis's emphasis is rightly on the European Union's denial of democracy, so that, for example, the popular will of the people of Greece against ever more austerity is ignored and traduced by the debilitating actions of the European Commission, European Central Bank and the International Monetary Fund, acting as a 'Troika'; a Russian word meaning 'set of three'.

DiEM launched itself in the Volksbühne (People's Theatre), not far from Alexanderplatz, once the centre of East Berlin. Atop the Volksbühne, a huge red banner was emblazoned with the Russian word 'nadriv', meaning 'anguish', reinforced by two large exclamation marks. Tsar Alexander the First visited Berlin in 1805, as Europe was convulsed by the Napoleonic Wars, to promote conservative alliances with Austria, Prussia and Britain against revolutionary France. Alexanderplatz was named in his honour, and the Russian flag still flutters over the massive Russian Embassy in nearby Unter den Linden, not far from the Brandenburg Gate.

So it is that geography as well as history continue to bind Russia and Germany, Europe's two largest economies. However, the first mention of Russia in DiEM's day of deliberations came in connection with Edward Snowden and his accidental safe haven there. Snowden and Julian Assange, who participated by video link in DiEM's public launch, have done much to reveal, via Wikileaks, how our world is run. Their commitment to transparency is reflected in DiEM's call for live-streaming of European Council meetings and related gatherings and actions. Might increased public scrutiny help to avert calamitous EU foreign policy initiatives such as the association agreement with Ukraine, which excludes Russia?

In April 2016, an advisory referendum on the European Union's association agreement with Ukraine was triggered in The Netherlands by popular demand, and the electorate voted against by almost two to one on a turnout of just over 30 per cent. The Dutch Government is obliged to take note of the outcome, which it had not sought. The Dutch referendum didn't figure in DiEM's day conference in Berlin. Indeed, there was little or no discussion of the EU's foreign policy and its troubled relationship with Russia, our close neighbour to the east.

Mass flight of refugees from Syria and elsewhere did figure in the press conference which preceded the day's discussions. Mr Varoufakis, Europe's best known finance minister, albeit he held the post only a few months, fielded questions about the tens of thousands of refugees then seeking safe harbour in Greece, the European Union's most proximate state to the Middle East. The previous day, Chancellor Merkel had been in Turkey meeting Prime Minister Davutoğlu and President Erdoğan. She complained how mostly Russian bombardments were driving new waves of refugees from northern Syria towards the border with Turkey. Meanwhile, the talks in Geneva between the Syrian government and its opponents teeter on the brink of collapse, while the ceasefire in Syria itself barely holds amidst daily breaches. During five long years, Syrians have died in their hundreds of thousands. Urgent humanitarian relief has been reaching some besieged communities. However, at the time of writing, Syria remains on a knife-edge, with continued killing and destruction combined with alarming signs of preparation for more armed intervention by Turkey, Saudi Arabia and others.

The geopolitics of this desperate situation didn't figure much in DiEM's day of discussion. Mr Varoufakis rightly pointed to the European Union's failure to address the mass migration as a collective, instead expecting Greece, Italy, Malta and other countries of arrival to deal with the huge influxes of people. Since then, the EU has entered into a shaming deal with Turkey that effectivey denies the rights of refugees under international law. Non-governmental organisations such as the Red Cross have suspended co-operation with the incarceration of refugees in camps in Greece. Further to the west, when some 500 people were drowned whilst attempting to cross the Mediterranean from Libya to Italy in April 2016, news coverage of this major tragedy was alarmingly small.

* * *

George Soros, the man who 'broke the Bank of England' on 'Black Wednesday' in 1992, has been explicit about Europe's precarious state. In an interview entitled 'The EU is on the verge of collapse' (*New York Review of Books*, 20.1.16), Mr Soros commented:

> ' ... There is plenty to be nervous about. As she [Chancellor Merkel] correctly predicted, the EU is on the verge of collapse. The Greek crisis taught the European authorities the art of muddling through one crisis after another. This practice is popularly known as kicking the can down the road, although it would be more accurate to describe it as kicking a ball uphill so that it keeps rolling back down. The EU now is confronted with not one but five or six crises at the same time.
>
> **Schmitz**: To be specific, are you referring to Greece, Russia, Ukraine, the coming British referendum, and the migration crisis?

Soros: Yes. And you haven't even mentioned the root cause of the migration crisis: the conflict in Syria. Nor have you mentioned the unfortunate effect that the terrorist attacks in Paris and elsewhere have had on European public opinion.

Merkel correctly foresaw the potential of the migration crisis to destroy the European Union. What was a prediction has become the reality. The European Union badly needs fixing. This is a fact but it is not irreversible. And the people who can stop Merkel's dire prediction from coming true are actually the German people. I think the Germans, under the leadership of Merkel, have achieved a position of hegemony. But they achieved it very cheaply. Normally hegemons have to look out not only for their own interests, but also for the interests of those who are under their protection. Now it's time for Germans to decide: do they want to accept the responsibilities and the liabilities involved in being the dominant power in Europe?'

This shrewd assessment was soon followed by another of Mr Soros' Russophobe outbursts. Writing in *The Guardian* (11.2.16), he declared:

'The leaders of the US and the EU are making a grievous error in thinking that president Vladimir Putin's Russia is a potential ally in the fight against Islamic State. The evidence contradicts them. Putin's aim is to foster the EU's disintegration, and the best way to do so is to flood Europe with Syrian refugees.'

This alarming if improbable theme was taken up by the *Financial Times*, which spoke of Russia and President Putin 'weaponising' the refugee issue.

'Our fragmenting Europe and DiEM's Response' was the theme of the morning's discussion in Berlin in February. Peace-building is difficult enough in the fraught state of regional affairs in the Mediterranean area, compounded by the simmering conflict in Ukraine. Many of those attending DiEM's birth in Berlin would probably be sympathetic to including this strand in the discussions. In fact, an SPD member of the Bundestag raised the distorting effect of increased defence spending to meet the US-set target of two per cent of gross domestic product. This was during the afternoon session on 'economic analysis and policy framework', chaired by Stuart Holland, whose article we feature.

Just as it needs democracy, so Europe needs its peace movement to find their voice. A major opportunity to do so will arise in Berlin in the autumn.

Yanis Varoufakis, Stuart Holland and Caroline Lucas MP look on as a speaker from Austria addresses Europe's political failure, in the Red Salon of Berlin's Volksbühne at the launch DiEM on 9 February 2016.

Beyond Austerity

Democratising Europe

Stuart Holland

Stuart Holland was a Labour MP for ten years before resigning his seat in 1989 to work with Jacques Delors, President of the European Commission. He prepared this paper for the launch of the Democracy in Europe Movement 2025 (DiEM25) in Berlin in February 2016, where he co-chaired with Yanis Varoufakis the session on economy. He develops the argument in his new book, Beyond Austerity: Democratic Alternatives for Europe *(Spokesman, £8.95), which shows how another Europe is possible.*

A precedent for DiEM25

The DiEM25 agenda is immensely ambitious. But an example relevant to its potential success was the campaign for European Nuclear Disarmament, during the 1980s, with its apocryphal acronym – END. Conceived and then mobilised across Europe principally by Ken Coates of the Bertrand Russell Peace Foundation, the END Appeal and its Conventions attracted tens of thousands of supporters, while its demonstrations mobilised hundreds of thousands across Europe in opposition to Cruise and Pershing medium range missiles and Soviet SS20s.

END distinguished itself from CND (Campaign for Nuclear Disarmament) in Britain in not only protesting against nuclear weapons, but also in stressing the feasibility of Europe as a non-nuclear security zone. Much as the DiEM25 (Democracy in Europe Movement) agenda is not only to protest against austerity, but also to demonstrate the feasibility of alternatives to it.

END was supported by a range of leading European politicians including, notably, Willy Brandt and Bruno Kreisky, as well as Neil Kinnock. With Robin Cook, I was a member of END's executive committee, and drew on it in making this case to the Soviet leadership before Neil's visit to Moscow as leader of the Labour Party, gaining their agreement to a joint declaration that if a Labour government insisted that the US withdraw Cruise missiles, they would not target Britain with SS20s, and would agree to joint site inspection to confirm this.

The Soviets accepted the feasibility of

Europe as a zone without medium range missiles since withdrawal of Cruise also was supported by the SPD in Germany at a time when Cruise missiles were deployed only in the UK, Germany and Italy. Within which there was a credible political and security logic. If the governments of two of these three countries would insist on their withdrawal, the third would be more likely to do so since it would not welcome being the only target for Soviet SS20s.

Through its combination of a mass protest movement, and political support, European Nuclear Disarmament thereby influenced the context, and credibility for the Soviets, of the 1987 Treaty on Intermediate Nuclear Forces (INF), which is the only one to successfully outlaw a whole class of missiles.

Not over her dead body

It is clear that Angela Merkel – as in her 2012 'over my dead body' declaration on Eurobonds – wrongly assumes that these must be guaranteed, underwritten and financed by German taxpayers. Yet European Investment Bank (EIB) bonds – since 1958 – never have been guaranteed by member states, nor serviced by them. Not that she is alone in displacing this.

At a meeting in Brussels in December 2014, neither the economic adviser to Council President Donald Tusk, nor the advisers to Jyrki Katainen, Commissioner for Investment and Growth, nor those to Marianne Thyssen, the Commissioner for Employment, nor the senior economic adviser to the Commission knew this. Whereas, it was immediately confirmed by Philippe Maystadt, a former president of the European Investment Bank.

This combines ignorance and incompetence. But it is highly relevant to realising the ambition of DiEM25 to achieve a European recovery. Even if, by a 'house rule' rather than treaty provision or statutory requirement, the European Investment Bank traditionally has only co-financed investments rather than financed them outright. Which was why, in a 1993 report on economic and social cohesion to Jacques Delors, President of the European Commission, I recommended a European Investment Fund whose bonds also need not count on national debt, and which was agreed and set up by the European Council in 1994 and which, since the 2000 Lisbon Agenda, has been part of the EIB group.

- Thereby, bonds issued by the European Investment Bank – and counterparted by the European Investment Fund – have the attributes of US Treasury Bonds, which do not count against the debt of the

American Union such as California or Delaware, but without needing fiscal federalism.

Incompetence in inventing unneeded new institutions

Besides this, the Commission has been incompetent in inventing a new and entirely unneeded European Fund for Strategic Investments to implement the Juncker 'recovery programme' by assuming that the European Investment Fund could only offer loan guarantees to small and medium enterprises (SMEs) rather than bond finance. This was an incompetent reading of the website of the EIF – for which an undergraduate or, certainly, a graduate student should be flunked – rather than a correct reading of its statutes. Which has more general relevance: institutions that have no memory of their own previous commitments invite a legitimation crisis. Which they now face.

Inconsistency, displacement and denial

In July 2014 Jean-Claude Juncker declared to the European Parliament that the top priority for his Presidency of the Commission would be a €300 billion bond-backed European Investment Bank 'recovery programme'. This was not accidental. In 2012 he had been invited by the Economic and Social Committee of the Union – representatives of employers, trades unions and civil society – to attend the public launch of its report claiming that economic recovery and social cohesion were feasible on the above lines.

By November 2014, President Juncker had allowed this programme to be slashed to €5 billion from the European Investment Bank plus recycling of some research funds in what otherwise is a private finance initiative (PFI) wish-list. A part-time committee then was appointed to decide what investment criteria for recovery should be, displacing that these were agreed for the European Investment Bank at Essen in 1994 to include Transport and Communications Networks – the TENS – and that the Amsterdam Special Action Programme of 1997 agreed a 'cohesion and convergence' remit for the EIB to include investments in health, education, urban regeneration, and safeguarding the environment – as well as support for SMEs.

Democratising decision-making

Inverting QMV by Enabling Majority Voting
Qualified Majority Voting means that member states in a majority weighted by population can bind others to adopt a policy irrespective of

the intent of their governments, the will of their parliaments, or the wishes of their electorates.

Giuliano Amato, a former prime minister of Italy, who was a vice-president of the Giscard d'Estaing Convention drafting the misbegotten Constitution for Europe, realised this risk and proposed alternative decision-making – Enabling Majority Voting or EMV rather than QMV. This could enable progress of joint policies by those governments ready to agree them on a majority basis, without imposing these on others which either disagreed or were not as yet ready to adopt them; as *de facto* had been the case with the introduction of the euro, which was agreed by some member states yet not imposed on others.

Giscard dismissed such Enabling Majority Voting out of hand. But with only a one clause Treaty amendment, it should enable any member state to call for an enabling majority vote if a qualified majority vote is moved by another or by others.

Remarkably, this has been displaced by David Cameron, since such a procedure can protect national democracy, and should be acceptable to the government of any member state. It would be the equivalent of De Gaulle's January 1966 'Luxembourg Compromise' by which any member state could reject a proposal that was not 'in the national interest' without inhibiting constructive common policies.

The proposal of such an enabling majority voting procedure, unlike qualified majority voting, also should allow it to be considered and accepted or rejected by national parliaments and, if it affects them, regional assemblies. Which, again, should attract support from governments who are concerned to convince electorates that Europe can reinforce democracy, rather than deny it.

Enhanced Cooperation
Until recently, 'enhanced cooperation' had been a footnote in treaties which near to no one ever read. Its main reference was to Schengen, which now is in total disarray in view of the refugee crisis. Yet although an enhanced cooperation procedure was not formally invoked at the time, the introduction of the euro itself was a de facto case of it since the euro was adopted by some members states without being imposed on others.

Nor could Germany now readily reject a wider use of enhanced cooperation in principle. She has invoked it in the proposal for a Financial Transactions Tax where the aim is to outflank David Cameron. If needed, it could be invoked to issue Eurobonds for recovery to outflank opposition to them from Germany.

Germany has gained the support of only 10 other member states for a Financial Transactions Tax. If invoked by France, Italy, Portugal and an anti-austerity coalition in Spain, issuing Eurobonds for recovery could well gain support from more, or most – not excluding the UK, granted George Osborne declaring in 2011 that he would support Eurobonds for recovery of the European Union since this was vital for British exports.

The power to govern they have but don't use

The European Council
The higher economic and financial authority either of the Eurozone or the wider European Union is not the Eurogroup or Eurozone finance ministers, nor the European Central Bank, but the European Council of heads of state and heads of government. The Council can define 'general economic policies' which can and should be those of a bond-based European recovery to fulfil Article 3 of the Treaties on the Functioning of the European Union, which includes the goals of high employment, sustained development and balanced growth. Thus Antonio Costa, before becoming prime minister of Portugal, with good reason had made the case that:

> 'We can't continue to have a Europe governed by finance ministers. We have to have a Europe governed by politicians. It's increasingly important that decisions are centred on the summits of heads of state and government, and less on the technicalities of finance ministers.'

The 'relative autonomy of the ECB'

It also has been widely displaced that the European Central Bank has a dual remit both to ensure the internal and external stability of the currency and, without prejudice to this, 'to support the general economic policies of the Union'. These terms of reference directly reflect those of the Bundesbank, i.e. *'die allgemeine Wirtschaftspolitik der Bundesregierung zu unterstützen'*. This reflected German concern to avoid inflation. But stability in terms of inflation now is not a problem, rather than major disinflation, plus risks of disintegration of the Eurozone itself. Notably, the governor of the National Bank of Austria, Ewald Nowotny, in June 2013, spelled out this dual remit of the ECB:

> 'In accordance with Article 127(1) and Article 282(2) of the Treaty on the Functioning of the European Union, the primary objective of the ESCB [The European System of Central Banks] shall be to maintain price stability. Without prejudice to the objective of price stability, it shall support the general economic policies in the Union with a view to contributing to the achievement

of the objectives of the Union as laid down in Article 3 of the Treaty on European Union.'

Nowotny therefore claimed that

'the primary task of monetary policy is to prevent inflation, but also deflation.'

He is right, and this should be cited and mobilised at a national and European level by DiEM activists.

DiEM25 and mobilising latent synergies

There also is the case for mobilising latent synergies with those who have a vested interest in alternatives to austerity, including not only trades unions and the institutions of civil society but also employers' federations, pension funds and sovereign wealth funds. This is consistent with the case made by Yanis Varoufakis in relation to our *Modest Proposal* in a conference address in Zagreb in May 2013. As he put it:

'When addressing diverse audiences ranging from radical activists to hedge fund managers, the idea is to forge strategic alliances even with right-wingers with whom we share a simple interest: an interest to end the negative feedback loop between austerity and crisis, between bankrupt states and bankrupt banks; a negative feedback effect that undermines both capitalism and any progressive programme for replacing it.'

Trades Unions and Employers' Federations
Synergies also are needed between anti-austerity governments and trades unions, but also with employers' federations. Not least since the Economic and Social Committee's 2012 *Restarting Growth* report not only was unanimously endorsed by German employers' representatives but also by all European employers' representatives on the committee, including Philippe de Beck, president of the European employers' federation, *Business Europe*.

Pension Funds
Similarly, Bill Gross when heading PIMCO, one of the world's largest pension funds with assets of over $1 trillion, also called for European recovery, stressing that pension funds needed growth to secure retirement incomes, whereas low to near zero interest rates in Europe would not enable a fund such as PIMCO to fund retirement incomes.

Sovereign Wealth Funds
Sovereign wealth funds have been damaged by the failure of Europe to gain an economic recovery. Thus, in March 2012, the Norwegian minister

of finance announced that Norway's sovereign wealth fund, the world's biggest and hitherto Europe's major institutional investor, would reduce its European commitments from over half to two-fifths while raising investments in emerging markets and Asia-Pacific from just over a tenth to two-fifths.

Yet, since when, growth in China has been slowing down, which increases the need for sovereign wealth funds to find investment outlets in Europe.

Rating Agencies

Such synergies should include briefing rating agencies. This may appear counterintuitive. Yet, while they can downgrade 'sovereign' debt, they cannot themselves govern. Thus, it has been widely overlooked that when Standard & Poor downgraded twelve Eurozone member states' debt in January 2012, it stressed that key reasons were simultaneous debt and spending reductions by governments and households, the weakening thereby of economic growth, and the transparent inability of European policymakers to agree what to do about it.

Key References

Economic and Social Committee (2012). *Restarting Growth: Two Innovative Proposals.* Brussels.

Holland, S. (2003). *How to Decide on Europe – Proposal for an Enabling Majority Voting Procedure in the European Constitution.* CEUNEUROP Discussion Paper no. 17. Faculdade de Economia, Universidade de Coimbra. July.

Holland, S. (2015). *Europe in Question – and what to do about it.* Paperback and eBook. Spokesman Books.

Nowotny, E. (2013). Opening remarks at the 41st Economics Conference of the Central Bank of the Republic of Austria. Vienna, June 10th.

Spiegel (2012). 'The Coming EU Summit Clash: Merkel Vows "No Euro Bonds as Long as I Live"'. http://www.spiegel.de/international/europe/chancellor-merkel-vows-no-euro-bonds-as-long-as-she-lives-a-841163.html. June 27th.

Varoufakis, Y. (2013). 'Confessions of an Erratic Marxist', conference address. Zagreb, May.

Varoufakis, Y., Holland, S. and Galbraith, J. K. (2014). *A Modest Proposal for Resolving the Eurozone Crisis 4.0.*

The 'short version' of DiEM25's Manifesto

A Manifesto for Democratising Europe

For all their concerns with global competitiveness, migration and terrorism, only one prospect truly terrifies the Powers of Europe: Democracy!

They speak in democracy's name but only to deny, exorcise and suppress it in practice. They seek to co-opt, evade, corrupt, mystify, usurp and manipulate democracy in order to break its energy and arrest its possibilities. For rule by Europe's peoples, government by the demos, is their nightmare.

The European Union could have been the proverbial Beacon on the Hill, showing the world how peace and solidarity may be snatched from the jaws of centuries-long conflict and bigotry. Alas, today, a common bureaucracy and a common currency divide European peoples that were beginning to unite despite our different languages and cultures.

Now, today, Europeans are feeling let down by EU institutions everywhere. From Helsinki to Lisbon, from Dublin to Crete, from Leipzig to Aberdeen. A stark choice is approaching fast. **The choice between authentic democracy and insidious disintegration.**

At the heart of our disintegrating EU there lies a guilty deceit: A highly political, top-down, opaque decision-making process is presented as 'apolitical', 'technical', 'procedural' and 'neutral'. Its purpose is to prevent Europeans from exercising democratic control over their money, communities, working conditions and environment.

The price of this deceit is not merely the end of democracy but also the dream of shared prosperity:
- The Eurozone economies are being marched off the cliff of competitive austerity, resulting in permanent recession in the weaker countries and low investment in the core countries
- EU member-states outside the Eurozone are alienated, seeking inspiration and partners in suspect quarters
- Unprecedented inequality, declining hope and misanthropy flourish throughout Europe

The more they asphyxiate democracy, the less legitimate their political authority becomes, the stronger the forces of economic recession, and the greater their need for further authoritarianism. Thus democracy's enemies gather renewed power while losing legitimacy and confining hope and prosperity to the very few (who may only enjoy it behind the gates and the fences needed to shield them from the rest of society).

This is the unseen process by which Europe's crisis is turning our peoples inwards, against each other, amplifying pre-existing jingoism, xenophobia. The privatisation of anxiety, the fear of the 'other', the nationalisation of ambition, and the re-nationalisation of policy threaten a toxic disintegration of common interests from which Europe can only suffer.

Europe's pitiful reaction to its banking and debt crises, to the refugee crisis, to the need for a coherent foreign, migration and anti-terrorism policy, are all examples of what happens when solidarity loses its meaning.

Two dreadful options dominate:
- Retreat into the cocoon of our nation-states
- Or surrender to the Brussels democracy-free zone

There must be another course. And there is!
It is the one official 'Europe' resists with every sinew of its authoritarian mind-set:
A surge of democracy!

Edmund Burke's line applies to today's Europe perfectly: 'The only thing necessary for the triumph of evil is that good people do nothing'. **Committed democrats must resolve to act across Europe.** With a view to call forth just such a surge, we are gathering on 9th February in Berlin to found a movement, **DiEM25.**

We come from every part of Europe and are united by different cultures, languages, accents, political party affiliations, ideologies, skin colours, gender identities, faiths and conceptions of the good society.

We come together as committed Europeans determined to prevent a clueless EU establishment, which is deeply contemptuous of democracy, from rendering impossible an authentically democratic European union.

One simple, radical idea is the motivating force behind **DiEM25:**
Democratise Europe!

The EU will either be democratised or it will disintegrate!
Our immediate priority is (A) full transparency in decision-making (e.g. live-streaming of European Council, Ecofin and Eurogroup meetings, full disclosure of trade negotiation documents, publication of ECB minutes etc.) and (B) the urgent redeployment of existing EU institutions in the pursuit of innovative policies that genuinely address the crises of debt, banking, inadequate investment, rising poverty and migration.

Our medium-term goal, once Europe's various crises have been stabilised, is to convene a constitutional assembly where Europeans will deliberate on how to bring forth, by 2025, a full-fledged European democracy, featuring a sovereign Parliament that respects national self-determination and sharing power with national Parliaments, regional assemblies and municipal councils.

We call on our fellow Europeans to join us forthwith to create DiEM25 and to fight together to democratise the European Union, to end the reduction of all political relations into relations of power masquerading as merely technical decisions; to subject the EU's bureaucracy to the will of sovereign European peoples; to dismantle the habitual domination of corporate power over the will of citizens; and to re-politicise the rules that govern our single market and common currency.

We are inspired by a Europe of Reason, Liberty, Tolerance and Imagination made possible by comprehensive Transparency, real Solidarity and authentic Democracy. **We aspire to:**

- A Democratic Europe in which all political authority stems from Europe's sovereign peoples
- A Transparent Europe where all decision-making takes place under the citizens' scrutiny
- A United Europe whose citizens have as much in common across countries as within them
- A Realistic Europe that sets itself the task of radical, yet achievable, democratic reforms
- A Decentralised Europe that uses central power to maximise democracy locally
- A Pluralist Europe of regions, ethnicities, faiths, nations, languages and cultures
- An Egalitarian Europe that celebrates difference and ends all forms of discrimination
- A Cultured Europe that harnesses its peoples' cultural diversity
- A Social Europe that recognises freedom from exploitation as a prerequisite for true liberty
- A Productive Europe that directs investment into a shared, green prosperity
- A Sustainable Europe that lives within the planet's means
- An Ecological Europe engaged in genuine worldwide green transition
- A Creative Europe that releases the innovative powers of its citizens' imagination
- A Technological Europe pressing new technologies in the service of solidarity
- A Historically-minded Europe that seeks a bright future without hiding from its past

- An Internationalist Europe that treats non-Europeans as ends-in-themselves
- A Peaceful Europe de-escalating tensions in its neighbourhood and beyond
- An Open Europe that is alive to ideas, people and inspiration from all over the world, recognising fences and borders as signs of weakness and sources of insecurity
- A Liberated Europe where privilege, prejudice, deprivation and the threat of violence wither, allowing Europeans to be born into fewer stereotypical roles, to enjoy even chances to develop their potential, and to be free to choose more of their partners in life, work and society.

Carpe DiEM25
www.diem25.org

United Nations · Designated
Educational, Scientific and · UNESCO Creative City
Cultural Organization · in 2015

Sailing from London to Russia in Elizabeth's cause.
Eisenstein's preparatory sketch for Ivan the Terrible, 1941.
©Russian State Archives of Literature and Art

Peaceful Means

Sergey Lavrov

Sergey Lavrov has served as Russia's Foreign Minister since 2004. Prior to that he was, for ten years, Russia's Permanent Representative to the United Nations. Our correspondent in Greece alerted us to this timely intervention, first published in Russia in Global Affairs.

International relations have entered a very difficult period, and Russia once again finds itself at the crossroads of key trends that determine the vector of future global development.

Many different opinions have been expressed in this connection including the fear that we have a distorted view of the international situation and Russia's international standing. I perceive this as an echo of the eternal dispute between pro-Western liberals and the advocates of Russia's unique path. There are also those, both in Russia and outside of it, who believe that Russia is doomed to drag behind, trying to catch up with the West and forced to bend to other players' rules, and hence will be unable to claim its rightful place in international affairs. I'd like to use this opportunity to express some of my views and to back them with examples from history and historical parallels.

It is an established fact that a substantiated policy is impossible without reliance on history. This reference to history is absolutely justified, especially considering recent celebrations. In 2015, we celebrated the 70th anniversary of Victory in World War Two, and in 2014 we marked a century since the start of World War One. In 2012, we marked 200 years since the Battle of Borodino and 400 years since Moscow's liberation from the Polish invaders. If we look at these events carefully, we'll see that they clearly point to Russia's special role in European and global history.

History doesn't confirm the widespread belief that Russia has always camped in Europe's backyard and has been Europe's political outsider. I'd like to remind you that the adoption of Christianity in Russia in 988 – we marked 1025 years of that event quite recently – boosted the development of state institutions, social relations and culture, and eventually made Kievan Rus a full member of the European community. At that time, dynastic marriages were the best gauge of a country's role in the system of international relations. In the 11th century, three daughters of Grand Prince Yaroslav the Wise became the queens of Norway and Denmark, Hungary and France. Yaroslav's sister married the Polish king, and his granddaughter married the German emperor.

Numerous scientific investigations bear witness to the high cultural and spiritual level of Rus of those days, a level that was frequently higher than in western European states. Many prominent Western thinkers recognized that Rus was part of the European context. At the same time, Russian people possessed a cultural matrix of their own and an original type of spirituality and never merged with the West. It is instructive to recall in this connection what was for my people a tragic and, in many respects, critical epoch of the Mongolian invasion. The great Russian poet and author Alexander Pushkin wrote: 'The barbarians did not dare to leave an enslaved Rus in their rear and returned to their Eastern steppes. Christian enlightenment was saved by a ravaged and dying Russia'. We also know an alternative view offered by prominent historian and ethnologist Lev Gumilyov, who believed that the Mongolian invasion had prompted the emergence of a new Russian ethnos and that the Great Steppe had given us an additional impetus for development.

However that may be, it is clear that the said period was extremely important for the assertion of the Russian State's independent role in Eurasia. Let us recall in this connection the policy pursued by Grand Prince Alexander Nevsky, who opted to temporarily submit to Golden Horde rulers, who were tolerant of Christianity, in order to uphold the Russians' right to have a faith of their own and to decide their fate, despite the European West's attempts to put Russian lands under full control and to deprive Russians of their identity. I am confident that this wise and forward-looking policy is in our genes.

Rus bent under but was not broken by the heavy Mongolian yoke, and managed to emerge from this dire trial as a single state, which was later regarded by both the West and the East as the successor to the Byzantine Empire that ceased to exist in 1453. An imposing country stretching along what was practically the entire eastern perimeter of Europe, Russia began a natural expansion towards the Urals and Siberia, absorbing their huge territories. Already then it was a powerful balancing factor in European political combinations, including the well-known Thirty Years' War that gave birth to the Westphalian system of international relations, whose principles, primarily respect for state sovereignty, are of importance even today.

At this point we are approaching a dilemma that has been evident for several centuies. While the rapidly developing Moscow state naturally played an increasing role in European affairs, the European countries had apprehensions about the nascent giant in the East and tried to isolate it whenever possible and prevent it from taking part in Europe's most important affairs.

The seeming contradiction between the traditional social order and a striving for modernisation based on the most advanced experience also dates back centuries. In reality, a rapidly developing state is bound to try and make a leap forward, relying on modern technology, which does not necessarily imply the renunciation of its 'cultural code'. There are many examples of Eastern societies modernising without the radical breakdown of their traditions. This is all the more typical of Russia that is essentially a branch of European civilisation.

Incidentally, the need for modernisation based on European achievements was clearly manifest in Russian society under Tsar Alexis, while talented and ambitious Peter the Great gave it a strong boost. Relying on tough domestic measures and resolute, and successful, foreign policy, Peter the Great managed to put Russia into the category of Europe's leading countries in a little over two decades. Since that time Russia's position could no longer be ignored. Not a single European issue can be resolved without Russia's opinion.

It wouldn't be accurate to assume that everyone was happy about this state of affairs. Repeated attempts to return this country into the pre-Peter times were made over subsequent centuries, but they failed. In the middle 18th century Russia played a key role in a pan-European conflict – the Seven Years' War. At that time, Russian troops made a triumphal entry into Berlin, the capital of Prussia under Frederick II, who had a reputation for invincibility. Prussia was saved from an inevitable rout only because Empress Elizabeth died a sudden death and was succeeded by Peter III, who sympathised with Frederick II. This turn in German history is still referred to as the Miracle of the House of Brandenburg. Russia's size, power and influence grew substantially under Catherine the Great when, as then Chancellor Alexander Bezborodko put it, 'Not a single cannon in Europe could be fired without our consent'.

I'd like to quote the opinion of a reputable researcher of Russian history, Hélène Carrère d'Encausse, the permanent secretary of the French Academy. She said the Russian Empire was the greatest empire of all times in the totality of all parameters – its size, an ability to administer its territories, and the longevity of its existence. Following Russian philosopher Nikolai Berdyayev, she insists that history has imbued Russia with the mission of being a link between the East and the West.

During at least the past two centuries, any attempts to unite Europe without Russia and against it have inevitably led to grim tragedies, the consequences of which were always overcome with the decisive participation of our country. I'm referring, in part, to the Napoleonic wars, upon the completion of which Russia rescued the system of international relations that was based on the balance of forces and mutual consideration for national interests, and ruled out the total dominance of one state in Europe. We remember that Emperor Alexander I took an active role in the drafting of decisions of the 1815 Vienna Congress that ensured the development of Europe without serious armed clashes during the subsequent 40 years.

Incidentally, to a certain extent the ideas of Alexander I could be described as a prototype of the concept on subordinating national interests to common goals, primarily, the maintenance of peace and order in Europe. As the Russian emperor said, 'there can be no more English, French, Russian or Austrian policy. There can be only one policy – a common policy that must be accepted by both peoples and sovereigns for common happiness'.

By the same token, the Vienna system was destroyed in the wake of the desire to marginalise Russia in European affairs. Paris was obsessed with this idea during the reign of Emperor Napoleon III. In his attempt to forge an anti-Russian alliance, the French monarch was willing, as a hapless chess grandmaster, to sacrifice all the other figures. How did it play out? Indeed, Russia was defeated in the Crimean War of 1853-1856, the consequences of which it managed to overcome soon due to a consistent and far-sighted policy pursued by Chancellor Alexander Gorchakov. As for Napoleon III, he ended his rule in German captivity, and the nightmare of the Franco-German confrontation loomed over Western Europe for decades.

Here is another Crimean War-related episode. As we know, the Austrian Emperor refused to help Russia, which, a few years earlier, in 1849, had come to his help during the Hungarian revolt. Then Austrian Foreign Minister Felix Schwarzenberg famously said: 'Europe would be astonished by the extent of Austria's ingratitude'. In general, the imbalance of pan-European mechanisms triggered a chain of events that led to the First World War.

Notably, back then Russian diplomacy also advanced ideas that were ahead of their time. The Hague Peace Conferences of 1899 and 1907, convened at the initiative of Emperor Nicholas II, were the first attempts to agree on curbing the arms race and stopping preparations for a devastating war. But not many people know about it.

The First World War claimed lives and caused the suffering of countless millions of people and led to the collapse of four empires. In this connection, it is appropriate to recall yet another anniversary, which will be marked next year – the 100th anniversary of the Russian Revolution. Today we are faced with the need to develop a balanced and objective assessment of those events, especially in an environment where, particularly in the West, many are willing to use this date to mount even more information attacks on Russia, and to portray the 1917 Revolution as a barbaric coup that dragged down all of European history. Even worse, they want to equate the Soviet regime to Nazism, and partially blame it for starting World War Two.

Without a doubt, the Revolution of 1917 and the ensuing Civil War were a terrible tragedy for our nation. However, all other revolutions were tragic as well. This does not prevent our French colleagues from extolling their upheaval, which, in addition to the slogans of liberty, equality and fraternity, also involved the use of the guillotine and rivers of blood.

Undoubtedly, the Russian Revolution was a major event which impacted world history in many controversial ways. It has become regarded as a kind of experiment in implementing socialist ideas, which were then widely spread across Europe. The people supported them, because wide masses gravitated towards social organisation with reliance on collective and community principles.

Serious researchers clearly see the impact of reforms in the Soviet Union on the formation of the so-called welfare state in Western Europe in the post-World War Two period. European governments decided to introduce unprecedented measures of social protection under the influence of the example of the Soviet Union in an effort to cut the ground from under the feet of the left-wing political forces.

One can say that the 40 years following World War Two were a surprisingly good time for Western Europe, which was spared the need to make its own major decisions under the umbrella of the US-Soviet confrontation, and enjoyed unique opportunities for steady development.

In these circumstances, Western European countries have implemented several ideas regarding conversion of the capitalist and socialist models, which, as a preferred form of socioeconomic progress, were promoted by Pitirim Sorokin and other outstanding thinkers of the 20th century. Over the past 20 years, we have been witnessing the reverse process in Europe and the United States: the reduction of the middle class, increased social inequality, and the dismantling of controls over big business.

The role that the Soviet Union played in decolonisation, and promoting international relations principles, such as the independent development of nations and their right to self-determination, is undeniable.

I will not dwell on the points related to Europe slipping into World War Two. Clearly, the anti-Russian aspirations of European elites, and their desire to unleash Hitler's war machine on the Soviet Union, played their fatal part here. Redressing the situation after this terrible disaster involved the participation of our country as a key partner in determining the parameters of the European and the world order.

In this context, the notion of the 'clash of two totalitarianisms,' which is now actively inculcated in European minds, including at schools, is groundless and immoral. The Soviet Union, for all its evils, never aimed to destroy entire nations. Winston Churchill, who all his life was a principled opponent of the Soviet Union and played a major role in going from the World War Two alliance to a new confrontation with the Soviet Union, said that graciousness, i.e. life in accordance with conscience, is the Russian way of doing things.

If you take an unbiased look at the smaller European countries, which previously were part of the Warsaw Treaty, and are now members of the European Union or NATO, it is clear that the issue was not about going from subjugation to freedom, which Western masterminds like to talk about, but rather a change of leadership. Russian President Vladimir Putin spoke about it not long ago. The representatives of these countries concede behind closed doors that they can't take any significant decision without the green light from Washington or Brussels.

It seems that in the context of the 100th anniversary of the Russian Revolution, it is important for us to understand the continuity of Russian history, which should include all of its periods without exception, and the importance of the synthesis of all the positive traditions and historical experience as the basis for making dynamic advances and upholding the rightful role of our country as a leading centre of the modern world, and a provider of the values of sustainable development, security and stability.

The post-war world order relied on confrontation between two world systems and was far from ideal, yet it was sufficient to preserve international peace and to avoid the worst possible temptation – the use of weapons of mass destruction, primarily nuclear weapons. There is no substance behind the popular belief that the Soviet Union's dissolution signified Western victory in the Cold War. It was the result of our people's will for change plus an unlucky chain of events.

These developments resulted in a truly tectonic shift in the international landscape. In fact, they changed global politics altogether, considering that the end of the Cold War and related ideological confrontation offered a unique opportunity to change the European architecture on the principles of indivisible and equal security and broad co-operation without dividing lines.

We had a practical chance to mend Europe's divide and implement the dream of a common European home, which many European thinkers and politicians, including President Charles de Gaulle of France, wholeheartedly embraced. Russia was fully open to this option and advanced many proposals and initiatives in this connection. Logically, we should have created a new foundation for European security by strengthening the military and political components of the Organisation for Security and Cooperation in Europe (OSCE). Vladimir Putin said in a recent interview with the German newspaper *Bild* that German politician Egon Bahr proposed similar approaches.

> … The will for peace must not be misunderstood or calumnied as a willingness to submit. The will for peace strives for a world in which each people may develop in safety and in respect for its neighbours, a world in which there are ideological conflicts which may be argued out by many means but definitely not by means of confrontation and violence. However, it seems we still have a long way to go until we reach this state …
>
> **Egon Bahr**
> *SPD Defence Spokesman, May 1982*
> *published in Spokesman 42*

Unfortunately, our Western partners chose differently. They opted to expand NATO eastward and to advance the geopolitical space they controlled closer to the Russian border. This is the essence of the systemic problems that have soured Russia's relations with the United States and the European Union. It is notable that George Kennan, the architect of the US policy of containment of the Soviet Union, said in his winter years that the ratification of NATO expansion was 'a tragic mistake'.

The underlying problem of this Western policy is that it disregarded the global context. The current globalised world is based on an unprecedented interconnection between countries, and so it's impossible to develop relations between Russia and the European Union as if they remained at the core of global politics as during the Cold War. We must take note of the powerful processes that are underway in Asia Pacific, the Middle East, Africa and Latin America.

Rapid change in all areas of international life is the primary sign of the current stage. Indicatively, they often take an unexpected turn. Thus, the concept of 'the end of history', developed by well-known US sociologist and political researcher Francis Fukuyama, that was popular in the 1990s, has become clearly inconsistent today. According to this concept, rapid globalisation signals the ultimate victory of the liberal capitalist model, whereas all other models should adapt to it under the guidance of the wise Western teachers.

In reality, the second wave of globalisation (the first occurred before World War One) led to the dispersal of global economic might and, hence, of political influence, and to the emergence of new and large centres of power, primarily in the Asia-Pacific Region. China's rapid upsurge is the clearest example. Owing to unprecedented economic growth rates, in just three decades it became the second and, calculated as per purchasing power parity, the first economy in the world. This example illustrates an axiomatic fact – there are many development models – which rules out the monotony of existence within the uniform, Western frame of reference.

Consequently, there has been a relative reduction in the influence of the so-called 'historical West' that was used to seeing itself as the master of the human race's destinies for almost five centuries. The competition on the shaping of the world order in the 21st century has toughened. The transition from the Cold War to a new international system proved to be much longer and more painful than it seemed 20-25 years ago.

Against this backdrop, one of the basic issues in international affairs is the form that is being acquired by this generally natural competition between the world's leading powers. We see how the United States and the US-led Western alliance are trying to preserve their dominant positions by any available method or, to use the American lexicon, ensure their 'global leadership'. Many diverse ways of exerting pressure, economic sanctions and even direct, armed intervention are being used. Large-scale information wars are being waged. Technology of unconstitutional change of governments by launching 'colour' revolutions has been tried and tested. Importantly, democratic revolutions appear to be destructive for the nations targeted by such actions. Our country, which went through a historical period of encouraging artificial transformations abroad, firmly proceeds from the preference of evolutionary changes that should be carried out in the forms and at a speed that conform to the traditions of a society and its level of development.

Western propaganda habitually accuses Russia of 'revisionism,' and the alleged desire to destroy the established international system, as if it was us who bombed Yugoslavia in 1999 in violation of the UN Charter and the

Helsinki Final Act, as if it was Russia that ignored international law by invading Iraq in 2003, and distorted UN Security Council resolutions by overthrowing Muammar Gaddafi's regime by force in Libya in 2011. There are many examples.

This discourse about 'revisionism' does not hold water. It is based on the simple and even primitive logic that only Washington can set the tune in world affairs. In line with this logic, the principle once formulated by George Orwell and moved to the international level, sounds like the following: all states are equal but some states are more equal than others. However, today international relations are too sophisticated a mechanism to be controlled from one centre. This is obvious given the results of US interference: there is virtually no state in Libya; Iraq is balancing on the brink of disintegration, and so on and so forth.

A reliable solution to the problems of the modern world can only be achieved through serious and honest co-operation between the leading states and their associations in order to address common challenges. Such an interaction should include all the colours of the modern world, and be based on its cultural and civilisational diversity, as well as reflect the interests of the international community's key components. We know from experience that when these principles are applied in practice, it is possible to achieve specific and tangible results, such as the agreement on the Iranian nuclear programme, the elimination of Syrian chemical weapons, the agreement on stopping hostilities in Syria, and the development of the basic parameters of the global climate agreement. This shows the need to restore the culture of compromise, the reliance on diplomatic work, which can be difficult, even exhausting, but which remains, in essence, the only way to ensure a mutually acceptable solution to problems by peaceful means.

Our approaches are shared by most countries of the world, including our Chinese partners, other BRICS (Brazil, Russia, India, China, South Africa) and Shanghai Co-operation Organisation (SCO) nations, and our friends in the Eurasian Economic Union (EAEU), the Collective Security Treaty Organisation (CSTO), and the Commonwealth of Independent States (CIS). In other words, we can say that Russia is fighting not against someone, but for the resolution of all the issues on an equal and mutually respectful basis, which alone can serve as a reliable foundation for a long-term improvement of international relations.

Our most important task is to join our efforts against, not some far-fetched, but very real challenges, among which terrorist aggression is the most pressing one. The extremists from ISIS, Jabhat al-Nusra and the like managed, for the first time, to establish control over large territories in

Syria and Iraq. They are trying to extend their influence to other countries and regions, and are committing acts of terrorism around the world. Underestimating this risk is nothing short of criminal shortsightedness.

The Russian President called for forming a broad-based front in order to defeat the terrorists militarily. The Russian Aerospace Forces make an important contribution to this effort. At the same time, we are working hard to establish collective actions regarding the political settlement of the conflicts in this crisis-ridden region.

Importantly, long-term success can only be achieved on the basis of movement to the partnership of civilisations based on respectful interaction of diverse cultures and religions. We believe that human solidarity must have a moral basis formed by traditional values that are largely shared by the world's leading religions. In this connection, I would like to draw your attention to the joint statement by Patriarch Kirill and Pope Francis, in which, among other things, they have expressed support for the family as a natural centre of life of individuals and society.

I repeat, we are not seeking confrontation with the United States, or the European Union, or NATO. On the contrary, Russia is open to the widest possible co-operation with its Western partners. We continue to believe that the best way to ensure the interests of the peoples living in Europe is to form a common economic and humanitarian space from the Atlantic to the Pacific, so that the newly formed Eurasian Economic Union could be an integrating link between Europe and Asia Pacific. We strive to do our best to overcome obstacles on that way, including the settlement of the Ukraine crisis caused by the coup in Kiev in February 2014, on the basis of the Minsk Agreements.

I'd like to quote the wise and politically experienced Henry Kissinger, who, speaking recently in Moscow, said that

> 'Russia should be perceived as an essential element of any new global equilibrium, not primarily as a threat to the United States ... I am here to argue for the possibility of a dialogue that seeks to merge our futures rather than elaborate our conflicts. This requires respect by both sides of the vital values and interest of the other.'

We share such an approach. And we will continue to defend the principles of law and justice in international affairs.

Speaking about Russia's role in the world as a great power, Russian philosopher Ivan Ilyin said that the greatness of a country is not determined by the size of its territory or the number of its inhabitants, but by the capacity of its people and its government to take on the burden of great world problems and to deal with these problems in a creative manner. A great power is one which, asserting its existence and its interest ... introduces a creative and meaningful legal idea to the entire assembly of the nations, the entire 'concert' of the peoples and states. It is difficult to disagree with these words.

© The Ministry of Foreign Affairs of the Russian Federation

The young Tsar

The Emperor Alexander, who was his own foreign minister, was quite a match for these able men. Metternich, Castlereagh, and Tallyrand all unsuccessfully tried to influence him; the King of Prussia followed him blindly, even against the advice of his own Ministers. In after years, it is true, Metternich acquired an ascendancy over the opinions of Alexander, but that belongs to a later phase of his character; in 1814 he still retained complete independence of judgement. He had learned diplomacy in a hard school. His grandmother was the enlightened and dissolute Catherine the Great; his father was the mad Tsar Paul. His grandmother took him away from his parents at birth, and saw to his education herself. Perceiving that Paul was not going to make a good Emperor, she wished to pass him over and make Alexander her successor. When he was not yet quite eighteen, his grandmother communicated this project to him in writing, and it was necessary for him to reply by letter. Placed thus between an aged autocrat and a frenzied psychopath, many boys would have difficulty in finding a suitable epistolary style. Not so Alexander. He wrote:

24 September 1796

Your Imperial Majesty!
I could never express my gratitude for the confidence with which your Majesty has been willing to honour me and the goodness which you have deigned to have in making by your own hand a writing serving as explanation of the other papers. I hope that your Majesty will see, by my zeal in deserving your precious favours, that I feel all their value. I could not, it is true, ever pay sufficiently, even by my blood, for all that you have deigned and still intend to do for me. These papers evidently confirm all the reflections which your Majesty has been good enough to communicate to me recently, and which, if it is permitted to me to say so, could not be more just. It is in placing once more at the feet of Your Imperial Majesty the sentiments of my most lively gratitude that I take the liberty of being, with the most profound respect and the most inviolable attachment, of Your Imperial Majesty the very humble and very submissive subject and grandson.

Alexander

Bertrand Russell attempted to trace the 'main causes' of political change during the hundred years from 1814 to 1914 in his book Freedom and Organization, *first published in 1934, from which this excerpt is taken.*

Sergey Eisenstein

Sergey Eisenstein

Gregory Woods

Gregory Woods' handsome new book, Homintern *(Yale, £25), has the subtitle* 'How Gay Culture Liberated the Modern World'. *This excerpt sketches some adventures of the great Soviet film director.*

Sergey Mikhailovich Eisenstein loved one man intensely for a long time. Grigori Alexandrov was a professional partner – as Eisenstein's assistant director – but probably not a sexual partner. Eisenstein's diaries of his 1926 trip to the fleshpots of Berlin, where he is known to have visited both gay male and lesbian nightclubs as well as Magnus Hirschfeld's Institute for Sexual Science, seem to contain coded erotic references to Alexandrov. According to the Polish writer Waclaw Solski, on one occasion when Eisenstein said that, unlike the Hollywood film-makers, he was not interested in girls, 'Grigori Alexandrov suddenly burst into a short laugh, but quickly stopped and turned red' – which proves nothing, since one can think of many reasons for his embarrassment at having let slip the laughter.

Eisenstein himself said to his biographer Marie Seton: 'A lot of people say I'm homosexual. I never have been, and I'd tell you if it were true.' But he did own up to having 'bisexual tendencies' in an 'intellectual way', like Balzac and Zola. In the United States in the early 1930s, he said to Joseph Freeman that, 'had it not been for Leonardo, Freud, Marx, Lenin and the movies, I would, in all probability, have been another Oscar Wilde'. Yet if these cultural and political distractions led him away from Wildedom, or compensated him for the repression of it, he had other cultural interests that might just as easily have had the opposite effect. For a start, he had a particular interest in Oscar Wilde himself. To promote the Proletkult Theatre's production of an adaptation of Jack London's *The Mexican*, which he had designed, Eisenstein adapted the publicity that had heralded Wilde's arrival in New York. When he went to London in November 1929, he later said, 'I found the authentic atmosphere of Oscar Wilde'. It seems to have been what he was looking for.

Eisenstein co-wrote a pantomime, *Columbine's Garter*, partly influenced by Jean Cocteau and Francis Poulenc's *Les Mariées de la Tour Eiffel*. He had a photograph of Cocteau, which he had cut out of the magazine *Je Sais Tout*, pinned to the wall in his flat. He must have been thrilled, then, to meet Cocteau when he went to Paris early in 1930; but embarrassed on the famous occasion a few nights later when he accompanied the Surrealist poet Paul Éluard to a performance of Cocteau's *La Voix humaine* at the Comédie Française, and Éluard shouted out at the traduced lover, on stage with her telephone, 'Who are you talking to? Monsieur Desbordes?' Jean Desbordes being Cocteau's then lover, this was intended, and taken, as a ribald joke at the expense of the author. A row broke out, and Éluard had to be ejected from the auditorium before the play could continue. Cocteau did not associate the offence, if any, with Eisenstein and when, a short while later, the Russian was threatened with deportation – he had fallen victim to a flurry of anti-Soviet feeling in France – both Cocteau and Colette supported him, even getting him a meeting with Philippe Berthelot, Director of the Ministry of Foreign Affairs. While still in Paris, Eisenstein frequented Sylvia Beach's bookshop Shakespeare and Company, where he was pleased to find Paul Verlaine's pornographic *Hombres* being sold, as he put it, 'under the counter quite openly'. He attended the salon of Marie-Laure de Noailles and was invited to visit her husband the vicomte in his villa at Hyères, but never actually got there. James Joyce gave him a signed copy of Ulysses, which had just come out; and Gertrude Stein, whom he met at Tristan Tzara's home, gave him advice on his imminent trip to the United States.

He does seem to have been one of those men whose homosexual aspect could flourish only when they were away from home. One biographer sums up his active sexual life as follows: 'It seems likely that Eisenstein experimented with homosexual sex – mainly with young men for money in Western Europe and Mexico – as well as occasionally sleeping with women, something he was pleased to hint at in his memoirs.' Travel took him to places where he found not only those young men but, perhaps more importantly, prominent cultural figures whom he respected and who were managing to live more or less openly with lovers of the same sex. Berlin, Paris and Wilde's London had all given him such glimpses of sexual and cultural possibility. As he set sail for New York on 8 May 1930, expecting

Alexandrov to follow a short while later, he is likely to have anticipated more of the same.

The New World gave him a prickly welcome, however. He was greeted with an anti-Semitic and anti-Communist campaign against his presence. In California he met Greta Garbo and watched Marlene Dietrich being directed by Josef von Sternberg, but his own dreams of film-making in Hollywood came to nothing. Instead, he went down to Mexico to make *Que Viva México!* with Upton Sinclair. Although the film was never completed by Eisenstein himself – it existed in three inferior versions until the 1970s, when Grigori Alexandrov managed to obtain the rushes and reconstruct a more plausibly Eisensteinian version – it contains what have been seen as striking moments of directorial self-revelation when the camera lingers on the bodies of oppressed peasant workers. Any analysis of its political message should take into account that, like Gide's *L'Immoraliste* or Thomas Mann's *Der Töd in Venedig*, this is a northern homosexual's southern text and has important things to express in that regard.

On 19 April 1932, Eisenstein set sail from New York on the *Europa*. The world of, if not the desire for, the Mexican peasant was left far in their wake as, for the duration of the crossing, he shared a table with those two cosmopolitan queens, Noël Coward and the critic and actor Alexander Woollcott. Meanwhile, some trunks that Eisenstein had sent to Hollywood from Mexico were opened by US Customs and found to contain many of his homosexually explicit drawings and a sheaf of photographs of male nudes. On 27 October 1934, he married Pera Attasheva, an actress and journalist. This was clearly a marriage of convenience: the couple lived separately and, far from their relationship's ever being consummated, Eisenstein himself said that they never so much as kissed. He did not even mention his wife in his memoirs. To an extent, if intended to mask his true sexuality, the marriage worked: the mere fact of his having a wife, albeit one he did not live with, gave the impression of a man who was heterosexual but chaste.

Rumours of homosexuality continued to surface, it seemed, whenever Eisenstein formed a close relationship with another man. For instance, when Paul Robeson spent a fortnight in Moscow at the end of 1934, he saw Eisenstein virtually every day, giving rise to a shiver of suggestive gossip. Similarly, there would be unfounded rumours about the relationship between Eisenstein and Nikolai Cherkassov, the star of his films *Alexander Nevsky* (1938) and *Ivan the Terrible* (1942-44, 1946). Of the films Eisenstein never made, among the more intriguing was a proposal for a piece about Lawrence of Arabia, whose complex psychology the director felt he might capture, like that of Ivan, in pure images. However, the career of Grigori Alexandrov, after the two men's return from the United States, gives an impression of the film-maker Eisenstein could never have become, despite some of his enthusiasms. Alexandrov successfully turned his hand to making Hollywood-style musicals for the entertainment of the masses. The nearest Eisenstein came to such work – although Alexandrov's first musical was a project which Eisenstein had himself turned down – was the closing reel, in colour, of *Ivan the Terrible*, which, if arguably camp in some respects, is more genuinely sinister in its raucous glamour than any musical comedy could have survived being.

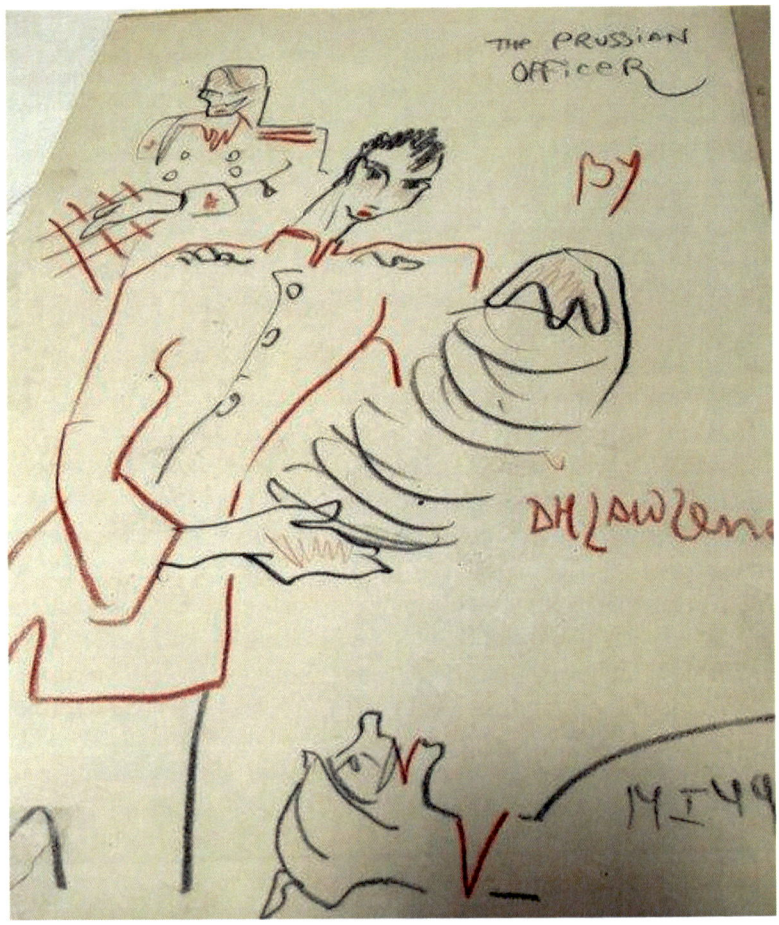

Eisenstein drawing inspired by D H Lawrence's short story
©Russian State Archives of Literature and Art

Eisenstein and Homintern

Anthony Lane

A recent London exhibition at the GRAD gallery highlighted the enduring appeal of a great Russian iconoclast, while a path-breaking new book situates Eisenstein's creative adventures in a broader context.

Gregory Woods has written an accessible, erudite and often amusing 'poet's book', which casts images 'on the reader's visual imagination, rather than persuade by linear argument'. Its mainspring encompasses the prejudice and suspicion inherent in homophobia, reflected in a poor if originally camp joke which spread to include some British gents who spied for the Soviet Union during the 1930s as forming a gay conspiracy or 'Homintern'. This was a double calumny on homosexuality and on international communism. The Communist International, or Comintern, dated back to 1919, and parties that wished to be admitted had to meet Lenin's 21 communist obligations.

Loyalty to the Comintern overrode all other commitments. So it was that the Cambridge communists included Guy Burgess, Anthony Blunt and James Klugmann, three gay men, plus bisexual Donald Maclean and heterosexual Kim Philby. Not that the Soviet affiliations of these five and others were necessarily mutually known. After Cambridge, Klugmann had the job of recruiting John Cairncross, 23 years old, who had started work at the Foreign and Commonwealth Office in 1937. The NKVD shrewdly chose the openly Communist Klugmann for the task, who was thought to be a more socially appealing to the modest Cairncross than Maclean, Burgess and other posh personages. Subsequently, during the Second World War, Cairncross spied at Bletchley Park, and the decoded intelligence on Nazi war plans in southern Russia that he passed to his Soviet minder probably altered the course of the fighting there. Defeat on the Eastern Front preceded defeats of Nazi Germany elsewhere. Cairncross, the 'fifth man', was 'straight', married twice and, like Klugmann, doesn't figure in Homintern's extensive index.

That these young men, and some women, became communists at Cambridge reflected the circumstances of the time. In the late 1920s and '30s, there was already a substantial anti-fascist movement in response to developments in Italy; and anti-imperialist sentiment railed against the conduct of the British and others in faraway China. The defeat of the General Strike in 1926, and the misery and desperation it engendered in mining and industrial communities across Britain, was deepened by the Crash of 1929 and the ensuing Depression. While Capitalism was collapsing, the Soviet Union was industrialising and collectivising its vast agriculture. The grass looked altogether greener, and principled young people risked all by committing themselves to spy for the Soviet Union.

The slur sometimes entailed in 'homintern' turns on conflating sexuality with 'treachery' as, for example, in Andrew Boyle's hatchet job, *The Climate of Treason*, published in 1979. In a characteristically infomative note, Woods writes:

> 'The spy books often pre-empt questions about the (un)trustworthiness of homosexual men by describing homosexuality in entirely negative terms. For instance, Andrew Boyle speaks of "the sad pleasures of sodomy" with specific reference to the exuberantly cheerful Guy Burgess; and characterises the "two most obvious weaknesses" of Donald Maclean as follows: "the first, an urge to drink himself into a stupor when depressed; the second and more repelling, a desire, in that condition, to consort with homosexuals".'

Boyle had interviewed Klugmann shortly before his death, who told him of the thrill at being involved in left-wing politics in Cambridge and Paris in the 1920s and 30s: 'It was a splendid time. The young can't begin to understand our sense of exhileration and adventurous freedom.' Their encounter is recounted in *The Shadow Man* (p.239) by Geoff Andrews (see *Spokesman 132*).

Woods ranges across continents, hemispheres and latitudes. He visits Harlem in the 1930s ('The New World'), where some young women found lesbian love, sometimes in exile from Europe and elsewhere, and Federica Garcia Lorca 'witnessed the Wall Street Crash in person'. He disentangles Henry Miller's homophobic comments on visiting Paris in the 1930s:

> 'One of the most famous of these American consumers of Parisian pleasures was Henry Miller. Prolifically engaged as he was, however, in what the city had to offer by way of heterosexual delicacies, his view of homosexual life in Paris

was fragmentary and only grudgingly acknowledged. Of a dance hall he might observe: "There were three or four whores at the bar and one or two drunks, English, of course. Pansies, most likely".'

Woods has a sharp eye for northern homosexuals accounts of southern love and vice versa. Russia receives generous and informative coverage.

Sergey Eisenstein, the pioneering and innovative Soviet film director, visited Europe in 1929-30, as recounted in the excerpt from *Homintern* reprinted in this issue of *The Spokesman*. Woods' hunch is that, when travelling, Eisenstein had more opportunity to explore his homosexual impulses, while somehow managing to survive Stalin's deadly purges on return to the Soviet Union. He was an astute, gifted and humorous artist, as 'Unexpected Eisenstein', the recent show at London's GRAD gallery, makes abundantly clear. The director's drawings for Rimbaud and Verlaine contort with desire, while those for 'Sherlock Holmes and Nick Carter' are altogether more straightlaced.

Eisenstein's last film, *Ivan the Terrible*, was made in the Soviet Union during the Second World War. It was left incomplete. The director planned a third part which would, among other things, explore Ivan's fantasies about Elizabeth I, the 'Virgin Queen' of England. They corresponded for more than two decades, as Elizabeth encouraged the development of trade

Elizabeth and the Boyar, Osip Nemeya: Eisenstein's drawing for Ivan the Terrible, 1942
©*Russian State Archives of Literature and Art*

via the Muscovy Company, while Ivan sought strategic alliances against Poland, Lithuania and others. But Eisenstein imagined a more carnal Elizabeth, turning the head of young Charles Blount and others. Certainly, in his sketches he has her more revealingly attired than anything usually seen in the chilly Elizabethan court. Some of these amusing drawings were on display in London at the GRAD gallery's excellent show. However, rumours of Ivan's proposal of marriage to Elizabeth seem unfounded. How different Anglo-Russian relations might have been!

Eisenstein's drawings of Constance and Mellors, inspired by Lawrence's *Lady Chatterley's Lover*, are altogether more sensuous and less comedic. They bring to mind Lawrence's own fine artwork, rarely seen. Eisenstein read the novel whilst sailing across the Atlantic. God only knows what he made of Mellors' Notts dialect ('Tha'rt not one o' them button-arsed lasses as should be lads, are ter!'), but Eisenstein was much taken with the 'naked' and what this revealed of the couple's inner lives. Such exploration of desire parallels Woods' own interests. For neither gay nor any other culture has yet much liberated the modern world.

Interestingly, Eisenstein's Lady Chatterley drawings feature in a short film by Mark Cousins commissioned for the exhibition at the GRAD, in which Cousins imagines a conversation he has with Eisenstein about Lawrence. This appealing short, complete with Cousins' Irish lilt, is paired with Derek Jarman's *Imagining October*, partly filmed in Moscow in 1984, when Jarman visited the Eisenstein Museum with other British directors including Sally Potter, who later cast Quentin Crisp as Elizabeth I and Tilda Swinton as Orlando in the film of the same name.

Homintern is comprehensively indexed, referenced and illustrated. It is beautifully written, printed, bound and jacketed. Yale University Press are to be commended for making available this pioneering work at an affordable price. Gregory Woods' hat-trick of titles for Yale represents a substantial addition to scholarship, knowledge and understanding.

www.yalebooks.co.uk
www.grad-london.com

Gregory Woods, *Homintern: How Gay Culture Liberated the Modern World*, Yale University Press, 2016, 438 pages, illustrated, hardback ISBN 9780300218039, £25

HOMINTERN

HOW GAY CULTURE LIBERATED THE MODERN WORLD

GREGORY WOODS

In this landmark international history, stretching from the Oscar Wilde scandal to the gay liberation movement, Gregory Woods explores how informal gay and lesbian networks effected seismic changes in twentieth-century culture.

'Woods' history of the 'homintern' is in turn hilarious and horrifying ... documents shocking levels of persecution. Homophobia was pervasive and vicious ... But this is not a gloomy book. Woods lovingly presents a range of gloriously outrageous gay and lesbian individuals and couples.'
– Joanna Bourke, *BBC History*

Hardback £25.00
24 black-and-white illustrations

YaleBooks | tel: 020 7079 4900
www.yalebooks.co.uk

Good Morning, Captain

The Captain counts destroyers –
Dauntless, Diamond, Decoy, Dragon,
corrals them one by one into his dock.
And when he's done destroyers, he starts on submarines –
Voracious, Venture, Vanguard, Vulpine, Vox.

And when the Captain dreams,
he dreams of all the things he's seen –
the fire on the glacier, explosions in the sea.
The Captain's been a hero. The Captain's done it all.
The Captain's got a lot of glitzy pins.

And when the Captain dreams,
the girls are wearing slinky things -
Emma, Lucy, Sarah, Charlotte, Claire.
The Captain's had his sweethearts. The Captain's seen it all.
The Captain's been the cat who got the cream.

And when the Captain dreams,
he dredges nightmares from the sea -
the slurpers and the suckers, the scuppered and the sunk.
They come with open mouths. They tick upon the hull.
They walk on crabby stilts and *whisper* things.

And when the Captain wakes,
he wonders why it's ten o clock,
and who put pastel flowers up the walls.
Good Morning, says the bedspread. *Good morning,* says his life,
the bloodknot sliding shut around his neck.

The Captain counts his children
from the photos in the albums,
thinks a thought, then chases it away.
And just on the horizon, tacking fast, the wind behind her,
that little speck that's closer every day

Abigail Parry

Silver bullets and neutron bombs

Alastair Crooke

Alastair Crooke is author of Resistance: The Essence of the Islamist Revolution *(Pluto Press, 2009).*

'The Americans did not act on what they promised in the nuclear accord [the Joint Comprehensive Plan of Action or JCPOA]; they did not do what they should have done. According to Foreign Minister [Javad Zarif], they brought something on paper but prevented materialisation of the objectives of the Islamic Republic of Iran through many diversionary ways,' the Supreme Leader, Khamenei, said in March, addressing a large group of people in the holy city of Mashhad. This sentence, uttered during the Supreme Leader's key *Nowruz* (New Year) address, should be understood as flashing amber light: it was no rhetorical flourish. And it was not a simple dig at America (as some may suppose). It was perhaps more of a gentle warning to the Iranian government to 'take care' of the possible political consequences.

What is happening is significant: for whatever motive, the US Treasury is busy emptying much of the JCPOA sanctions relief of any real substance (and their motive is something which deserves careful attention). The Supreme Leader also noted that Iran is experiencing difficulties in repatriating its formerly frozen, external funds.

US Treasury officials, since 'implementation' day, have been doing the rounds, warning European banks that the US sanctions on Iran remain in place, and that European banks should not think, even for a second, of tapping the dollar or euro bond markets in order to finance trade with Iran, or to become involved with financing infrastructure projects in Iran. Banks well understand the message: touch Iranian commerce and you will be whacked with a billion dollar fine – against which there is no appeal, no clear legal framework – and no argument countenanced. The banks (understandably) are shying off. Not a single bank or financial lending institution turned up when President Rouhani visited Paris, to hold meetings with the local business élite.

The influential *Keyhan* Iranian newspaper wrote on 14 March on this matter: 'Speaking at the UN General Assembly session in September, Rouhani stated: "Today a new phase of relations has started in Iran's relations with the world". He also stated in a live radio and television discussion with the people on *Tir:* "The step-by-step implementation of this document could slowly remove the bricks of the wall of mistrust".' *Keyhan* continues:

> 'These remarks were made at a time when the Western side, headed by America, does not have any intention to remove or even shorten the wall of mistrust between itself and Iran ... Moreover, they are delaying the implementation of their JCPOA commitments. Lifting the sanctions has remained *merely as a promise on a piece of paper*, so much so that it has roused the protest of Iranian politicians.
>
> The American side is promoting conditions in such a way that today even European banks and companies do not dare to establish financial relations with Iran – since all of them fear America's reaction in the form of sanctions [imposed on those same banks]. Actually, the reason for the delay in the commencement of the European banks' financial co-operation with the Iranian banks and the failure to facilitate banking and economic transactions, is because many of the American sanctions are still in place, and Iranian banks' financial transactions are [still] facing restrictions. Moreover, given their continuing fear of the biting legislations and penalties for violations of the Americans' old sanctions, European financial institutions are concerned about violating the American sanctions that continue to be in force ...
>
> It is pointless to expect the US administration to co-operate with Iran given the comments of the US officials, including Susan Rice, since the Americans' comments and behaviour reveal their non-compliance with their obligations and speak of the absence of the US administration's political will to implement even its minimum obligations.'
>
> [Here *Keyhan* is specifically referring to Susan Rice's observation to Goldberg in *The Atlantic* that, 'The Iran deal was never primarily about trying to open a new era of relations between the US and Iran. The aim was very simply to make a dangerous country less dangerous. No one had any expectation that Iran would be a more benign actor.']
>
> *Any action on the international scene calls for suitable and appropriate reaction.* Therefore, we cannot expect a government like the US administration that seizes every single opportunity to restrict our county, to lift the sanctions.

Rice's recent comments are only a small part of the increasing anti-Iranian rhetoric of the American officials in recent months. These remarks should actually be regarded as a sign ... that the dream of the JCPOA is nothing but wishful thinking and far from reality.' (Emphasis added).

The Supreme Leader's nudge, therefore, was intended for the ears of the government: do not build too much politically on this accord: beware its foundations may turn out to be built on sand.

Recently, US Treasury Secretary Jacob Lew gave a talk at *Carnegie* on the 'Evolution of Sanctions and Lessons for the Future', on which David Ignatius of the *Washington Post* commented:

> 'Economic sanctions have become the "silver bullet" of American foreign policy over the past decade, because they're cheaper and more effective in compelling adversaries than traditional military power. But Jack Lew warns of a "risk of overuse" that could neuter the sanctions weapon and harm America. His caution against overuse comes as some Republican members of Congress are fighting to maintain US sanctions on the Iranian nuclear program despite last year's deal limiting that Iranian threat.'

So what is going on here? If Lew is warning against sanction overreach, why is it that it is precisely his department that is the one that is so assiduously undermining sanctions relief for Iran – 'particularly since Lew's larger point is that sanctions won't work if countries don't get the reward they were promised – in the removal of sanctions – once they accede to U.S. Demands', in the paraphrase by Ignatius himself? One reason for this apparent contradiction implicit in Lew's remarks probably is China: recall that when China's stock markets were in freefall and haemorrhaging foreign exchange, as it sought to support the Yuan – China blamed the US Fed (US Reserve Bank) for its problems – and promptly was derided for making such an 'outlandish' accusation. Actually, what the Fed was then doing was stating its intent to raise interest rates (for the best of motives naturally!) – just as those, such as Goldman Sachs, have been advising. US corporate and bank profits are sliding badly, and in 'times of financial depletion', as the old adage goes, 'bringing capital home becomes the priority' – and a strong dollar does exactly that.

But the Peoples' Bank of China (PBOC) did a bit more than just whinge about the Fed actions, it reacted: *it allowed the Yuan to weaken,* which induced turmoil across a global financial world (already concerned about China's economic slowing); then raised the Yuan value to squeeze out speculation, betting on further falls in the Yuan; then let it weaken again as the Fed comments started to slide in favour of interest rate hikes, and a strong dollar – until finally, as *Zero Hedge* [financial analysis website] has noted,

> 'it appeared the messaging from The People's Bank Of China to The Fed was heard loud and understood. Having exercised its will to weaken the Yuan (implying turmoil is possible), Janet Yellen (Fed Chair) delivered the dovish goods [i.e. indicated that global conditions trumped the advice of the likes of Goldman Sachs to strengthen the dollar], and so China "allowed" the Yuan to rally back. In a double-whammy for everyone involved, the biggest 3-day strengthening of the Yuan fix since 2005 also pushed the Yuan forwards, back to their richest relative to spot since August 2014 – once again showing their might against the dastardly speculative shorts.'

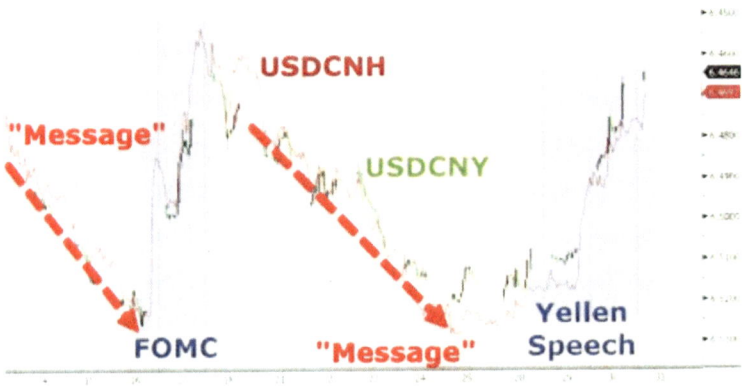

Zerohedge: And since Janet delivered, PBOC has strengthened the Yuan Fix by the most since 2005!

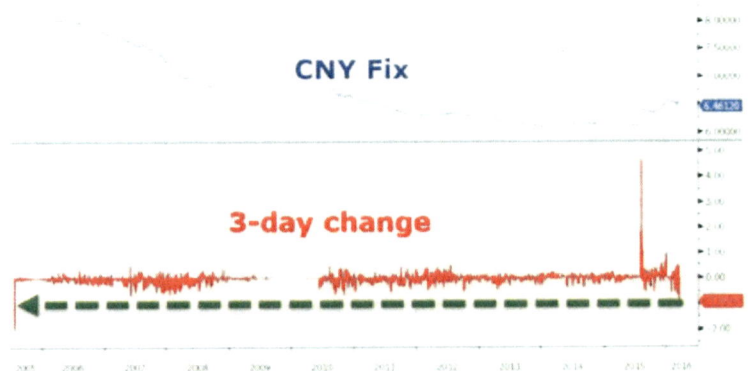

Zerohedge: Crushing shorts as Yuan forwards collapse back to their 'richest' relative to spot since August 2014.

Source of three graphs: Zerohedge

In short, the Ignatius 'silver bullet' of foreign policy (the US Treasury Wars against any potential competitor to US political or financial hegemony) is facing growing 'hybrid' financial war, just as NATO has been complaining that it is having to adjust to 'hybrid' conventional war – from the likes of Russia. So, as the US tries to expand its reach, for example by claiming legal jurisdiction over the Bank of China, and by blacklisting one of China's largest telecom companies, thus forbidding any US company from doing business with China's ZTE, China is pushing back. It has just demonstrated convincingly that US Treasury 'silver bullets' can fall short. This, we think, may have been Lew's point – one directed, possibly, at Congress, which has become truly passionate about its new found 'neutron bomb' (as a former Treasury official described its geo-financial warfare).

In respect to Russia, this is important: Russia and America seem to be edging towards some sort of 'grand bargain' over Syria (and possibly Ukraine, too), which is likely to involve the Europeans lifting, in mid 2016, their sanctions imposed on Russia. But again, the US is likely nonetheless to maintain its own sanctions (or even add to them, as some in the US Congress are arguing). So, if Russia, like Iran and China, become disenchanted with promises of US sanctions relaxation – then, as the *Keyhan* author noted, a suitable and appropriate (i.e. adverse) reaction, will ensue.

What the Fed and Lew seem to have assimilated is that the US and European economies are now so vulnerable and volatile that China and Russia can, as it were, whack back at America – especially where China and Russia co-ordinate strategically. Yellen specifically signalled 'weakening world growth' and 'less confidence in the renormalization process' as reasons for the Fed backtrack.

Ironically, David Ignatius in the *Washington Post* (29.03.16) gives the game away: Lew is not going soft, saying that the US needs to use its tools more prudently; far from it. His point is different, and Ignatius exposes it inadvertently:

> 'US power flows from our unmatched military might, yes. But in a deeper way, it's a product of the dominance of the US economy. Anything that expands the reach of US markets – such as the Trans-Pacific Partnership in trade, for example – adds to the arsenal of US power. Conversely, US power is limited by measures that drive business away from America, *or allow other nations to build a rival financial architecture that's less encumbered by a smorgasbord of sanctions.*'

This latter point precisely is what is frightening Lew and Ignatius. The tables are turning: in fact, the US and Europe may be becoming more vulnerable to retaliation (e.g. Europe, with Russia's retaliatory sanctions on European agricultural products) than China and Russia are to unilateral Treasury or Fed warfare. *This is the new hybrid war* (and not the hot air issuing from NATO). Lew and Ignatius know that a parallel 'architecture' *is* under construction, and that Congress's addiction to new sanctions is just speeding it into place.

So, why then is the US Treasury so zealous in undermining the effectiveness of JCPOA's agreed lifting of sanctions? Well, probably because Iran has less leverage over the global financial system than either China or Russia. But also, perhaps, because 'Iran sanctions' are (erroneously) viewed by US leaders as the Treasury's 'jewel in its crown' of geo-financial success.

What may be missing from this hubristic interpretation, however, is the understanding that Iran's experience will not be lost on the others, nor on the Shanghai Co-operation Organisation when it convenes its next meetings on how to combat western 'colour revolution' operations (with Iran likely joining that organisation as a member, rather than an observer, this summer).

Re-printed with permission
www.conflictsforum.org

Political responsibility in the nuclear age

An open letter to the American people

Richard Falk
David Krieger
Robert Laney

The authors are affiliated with the Santa Barbara - based Nuclear Age Peace Foundation.

Dear fellow citizens,

By their purported test of a hydrogen bomb early in 2016, North Korea reminded the world that nuclear dangers are not an abstraction, but a continuing menace that the governments and peoples of the world ignore at their peril. Even if the test were not of a hydrogen bomb but of a smaller atomic weapon, as many experts suggest, we are still reminded that we live in the Nuclear Age, an age in which accident, miscalculation, insanity or intention could lead to devastating nuclear catastrophe.

What is most notable about the Nuclear Age is that we humans, by our scientific and technological ingenuity, have created the means of our own demise. The world currently is confronted by many threats to human wellbeing, and even civilisational survival, but we focus here on the particular grave dangers posed by nuclear weapons and nuclear war.

Even a relatively small nuclear exchange between India and Pakistan, with each country using 50 Hiroshima-size nuclear weapons on the other side's cities, could result in a nuclear famine killing some two billion of the most vulnerable people on the planet. A nuclear war between the US and Russia could destroy civilisation in a single afternoon and send temperatures on Earth plummeting into a new ice age. Such a war could destroy most complex life on the planet. Despite the gravity of such threats, they are being ignored, which is morally reprehensible and politically irresponsible.

We in the United States are in the midst of hotly contested campaigns to determine the candidates of both major political parties in the 2016 presidential face-off, and yet none of the frontrunners for the nominations have even voiced concern about the nuclear war dangers we face. This is an appalling oversight. It reflects the underlying situation of denial and complacency that disconnects the American people as a whole from the risks of use of nuclear weapons in the years ahead. This menacing disconnect is reinforced by the media, which has failed to challenge the candidates on their approach to this apocalyptic weaponry during the debates and has ignored the issue in their television and print coverage, even to the extent of excluding voices that express concern from their opinion pages. We regard it as a matter of urgency to put these issues back on the radar screen of public awareness.

We are appalled that none of the candidates running for the highest office in the land has yet put forward any plans or strategy to end current threats of nuclear annihilation, none has challenged the planned expenditure of $1 trillion to modernise the US nuclear arsenal, and none has made a point of the US being in breach of its nuclear disarmament obligations under the Nuclear Non-Proliferation Treaty. In the presidential debates it has been a non-issue, which scandalises the candidates for not raising the issue in their many public speeches and the media for not challenging them for failing to do so. As a society, we are out of touch with the most frightening, yet after decades still dangerously mishandled, challenge to the future of humanity.

There are nine countries that currently possess nuclear weapons. Five of these nuclear-armed countries are parties to the Nuclear Non-Proliferation Treaty (US, Russia, UK, France and China), and are obligated by that treaty to negotiate in good faith for a cessation of the nuclear arms race and for nuclear disarmament. The other four nuclear-armed countries (Israel, India, Pakistan and North Korea) are subject to the same obligations under customary international law. None of the nine nuclear-armed countries has engaged in such negotiations, a reality that should be met with anger and frustration, and not, as is now the case, with indifference. It is not only the United States that is responsible for the current state of denial and indifference. Throughout the world there is a false confidence that, because the Cold War is over and no nuclear weapons have been used since 1945, the nuclear dangers that once frightened and concerned people can now be ignored.

Rather than fulfil their obligations for negotiated nuclear disarmament, the nine nuclear-armed countries all rely upon nuclear deterrence and are engaged in modernisation programs that will keep their nuclear arsenals active through the 21st century and perhaps beyond. Unfortunately, nuclear deterrence does not actually provide security to countries with nuclear arsenals. Rather, it is a hypothesis about human behaviour, which is unlikely to hold up over time. Nuclear deterrence has come close to failing on numerous occasions and would clearly be totally ineffective, or worse, against a terrorist group in possession of one or more nuclear weapons, which has no fear of retaliation and may actually welcome it. Further, as the world is now embarking on a renewed nuclear arms race, disturbingly reminiscent of the Cold War, rising risks of confrontations and crises between major states possessing nuclear weapons increase the possibility of use.

As citizens of a nuclear-armed country, we are also targets of nuclear weapons. John F. Kennedy saw clearly that

'Every man, woman and child lives under a nuclear sword of Damocles, hanging by the slenderest of threads, capable of being cut at any moment by accident, or miscalculation, or by madness. The weapons of war must be abolished before they abolish us.'

What President Kennedy vividly expressed more than 50 years ago remains true today, and even more so as the weapons proliferate and as political extremist groups come closer to acquiring these terrible weapons.

Those with power and control over nuclear weapons could turn this planet, unique in all the universe in supporting life, into the charred remains of a Global Hiroshima. Should any political leader or government hold so much power? Should we be content to allow such power to rest in any hands at all?

It is time to end the nuclear weapons era. We are living on borrowed time. The US, as the world's most powerful country, must play a leadership role in convening negotiations. For the US to be effective in leading to achieve Nuclear Zero, US citizens must awaken to the need to act and must press our government to act and encourage others elsewhere, especially in the other eight nuclear-armed countries, to press their governments to act as well. It is not enough to be apathetic, conformist, ignorant or in denial. We all must take action if we want to save humanity and other forms of life from nuclear catastrophe. In this spirit, we are at a stage where we need a robust global solidarity movement that is dedicated to raising awareness of the growing nuclear menace, and the urgent need to act nationally, regionally and globally to reverse the strong militarist currents that are pushing the world ever closer to the nuclear precipice.

Nuclear weapons are the most immediate threat to humanity, but they are not the only technology that could play and is playing havoc with the future of life. The scale of our technological impact on the environment (primarily fossil fuel extraction and use) is also resulting in global warming and climate chaos, with predicted rises in ocean levels and many other threats – ocean acidification, extreme weather, climate refugees and strife from drought – that will cause massive death and displacement of human and animal populations.

In addition to the technological threats to the human future, many people on the planet now suffer from hunger, disease, lack of shelter and lack of education. Every person on the planet has a right to adequate nutrition, health care, housing and education. It is deeply unjust to allow the rich to grow richer while the vast majority of humanity sinks into deeper poverty. It is immoral to spend our resources on modernising weapons of mass annihilation while large numbers of people continue to suffer from the ravages of poverty.

Doing all we can to move the world to Nuclear Zero, while remaining responsive to other pressing dangers, is our best chance to ensure a benevolent future for our species and its natural surroundings. We can start by changing apathy to empathy, conformity to critical thinking, ignorance to wisdom, denial to recognition, and thought to action in responding to the threats posed by nuclear weapons and the technologies associated with global warming, as well as to the need to address present human suffering arising from war and poverty.

The richer countries are challenged by migrant flows of desperate people that number in the millions and by the realisation that as many as a billion people on the planet are chronically hungry and another two billion are malnourished, resulting in widespread growth stunting among children and other maladies. While ridding the world of nuclear weaponry is our primary goal, we are mindful that the institution of war is responsible for chaos and massive casualties, and that we must also challenge the militarist mentality if we are ever to enjoy enduring peace and security on our planet.

The fate of our species is now being tested as never before. The question before us is whether humankind has the foresight and discipline necessary to forego some superfluous desires, mainly curtailing propensities for material luxuries and for domination of our fellow beings, thereby enabling all of us and succeeding generations to live lives worth living. Whether our species will rise to this challenge is uncertain, with current evidence not reassuring.

The time is short and what is at risk is civilisation and every small and great thing that each of us loves and treasures on our planet.

www.wagingpeace.org

Ireland's Guantanamo Granny

Margaretta D'Arcy

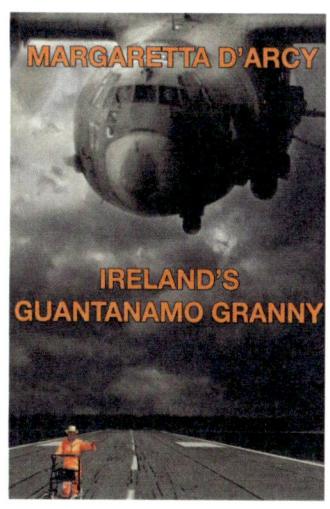

On Easter Sunday, 2016, the centenary of Ireland's Easter Rising and its Proclamation of Independence from British rule, a US Navy C-130T Hercules aircraft was under Irish guard at Shannon Airport. Not that it had been detained by the Irish authorities for compromising Irish neutrality in international relations. Rather, it was the latest in a long line of US military flights, carrying cargoes unknown, stopping over en route to war and rendition hotspots in the Middle East and elsewhere. The Irish authorities were protecting the aircraft from inspection by Irish citizens such as Margaretta D'Arcy and her colleagues in Shannonwatch, who have long campaigned to highlight Ireland's illegal collusion in conflicts worldwide. Following a short walk on the runway at Shannon, Margaretta, age 82 years, was eventually sent to Limerick Jail in January 2014. She recounts her experience there in this excerpt from Ireland's Guantanamo Granny, *her recently published account of unfinished business on Ireland's Atlantic coast (Women's Pirate Press, ISBN 9780952820611).*

Limerick Jail

'The Irish prison governor has no control over the number of prisoners being committed to jail, no control over the numbers of prisoners accommodated in his prison any day or night, no power to transfer or release prisoners out of his prison, no power to refuse to take prisoners ... no control over the number of staff assigned to his prison, no control over the staff assigned to search prisoners and visitors.'

John Lonergan, The Governor

The Irish Prison Board has a centralised bureaucratic approach to management. It has no authority. All authority rests with the Minister of Justice Dysfunction.

When I arrive at the office to the women's section of Limerick Jail, the elderly, grey-haired prison officer says: 'You'll be out in a couple of hours, just sign the bond and you're out'. 'Will it have Shannon on it?' I ask. 'Oh no, it's just the general one you sign at the garda station to keep the law.' 'That would be no problem for me,' I say. 'I normally keep the law, going on the runway was keeping the law.' 'Just wait and it will be sorted out,' she says. My heart lifts. I can catch the bus home. I have my travel pass. I'll be home in a couple of hours.

I'm in a small waiting room for children visiting their mothers, toys in one corner. 'Can I leave the door open so I can see out?' I ask. I see the women coming in to visit, babies in their arms, staff arriving, a building site in the middle for a new men's wing. In half an hour the prison officer returns. The Department says no. 'Is that Shatter?' I ask. It is very curious that at no time am I shown the bond paper. As I go to be processed in the office a sheepish group of well-dressed people and a priest pass me by, they must be the prison visitors. They pretend not to notice me or the other woman sitting there. A young prison officer comes through the door and leads me away into the bowels of the jail. We wind our way through a labyrinth of stairs and corridors, eventually arriving at the reception area.

I am brought into the receiving office. There is another woman there, middle-aged. We sit beside each other. I think she must be a prison officer but no, she is being processed for not paying a TV licence fee. She has five children, her son lives with her. She was exempted from the fee because she was disabled but now her son is living with her she has to pay. I never see her again and wonder if she got temporary release.

Wilfred Scawen Blunt noted in 1888 while serving time as a political prisoner in Galway Jail: 'There had been a pleasant feeling between prisoners and wardens due to the fact that they were much of the same class, peasants born, with the same natural ideas, virtues, vices and weaknesses.' It feels pretty much the same today.

My watch is taken along with the rest of my few belongings: phone, purse, travel card. From now on they own my time. There are no clocks in the jail so we never know the time but rely on the prison officers' word when we are locked up or let out. We are allowed one phone call of six minutes every day, one visit a week. We have to call officers by their surname.

Miss D studied at university. When she left she took temporary work as a prison officer and has stayed ever since – she needs the money. Her advice to me is: 'Don't believe everything you hear from a prisoner and keep your cell locked when you leave'. Otherwise it is pretty much like being in a boarding school. When asked the age of the prisoners, to my surprise she says they are on average about 40. She lets slip that they have the largest illegal cannabis house-grower in Ireland awaiting trial, she is Vietnamese.

Limerick was built as a high security jail. It was never meant to be a women's jail so the women are shunted off to a corner far from the main building, more like a dungeon with dark narrow corridors. I am on the ground floor. There are four cells, then a cell for the prison officers. It's all cooped up. Nothing like the grandeur of Armagh or even the open spaces in Holloway, not even India was so cramped.

My cell is a narrow space with the window blocked out leaving a tiny dial in the stone wall, which I can open to get some air through the grids. Wood broken down from what looks like packing cases is nailed together for a cupboard which also serves as a table. A steel barrier separates the wash basin and the toilet (also steel, no lid) from the bed and eating place. There are two bunk beds, mine is the bottom one. There is a small TV (no remote), a kettle and a radio.

Learning the Ropes

I am not given any details about the routine of prison life. 'You'll catch on,' I'm told. I sit there. No bedding. I think that the reason for giving no information is that I will need to rely on the other prisoners to show me the ropes. You earn brownie points for integrating with one's cellmates: it is one of the criteria for early release. Going on courses also earns brownie points. You get paid €1.75 a day, more if you are serving longer than a month, extra for working, that is sweeping and cleaning the corridors, serving food, taking the laundry to the washing machine.

I am locked in. After a while the door opens. Bedding, clean clothes, tracksuit, t-shirt, runners, toothbrush, soap, plastic plate, and a plastic knife and fork are brought in by a prisoner who tells me it's teatime. I join the queue. Someone helps me up the narrow stairs as I need to use a stick. There are cells upstairs. I pass them and go through a door where I see women with trays. We line up. On coming in, I said I was vegetarian. A cardboard plate is given to me with a salad, some bread, two tabs of butter and a carton of milk. There is a basket full of tea bags, another of sugar sachets and one with jam and marmalade. A row of officers flank the exit. A young woman is serving: she has a black eye. No one speaks. The line moves along. A woman asks if I need help to go down the stairs. I manage alone.

I am locked up. After a while the door is unlocked again. I go out into a narrow yard flanked by the grey prison walls, with a couple of picnic tables and a small shelter. It is cold. Fortunately, before I left the house I grabbed a warm coat and a woolly cap – a woman says I'm lucky to be able to wear a cap. Hoodies are forbidden. It seems most of the 28 or so women prisoners are here. They surround me and seem to know my business. They think I'm mad not to have signed the bond. They feel quite aggrieved as if I am demeaning them by having a choice; they didn't have a choice. For a moment I think there might be a mini riot and they will go to the Governor and ask for my removal as not being suitable to be with them. Who was I to try and get rid of the Americans – they are needed in case of war. I am surrounded.

Who has told them? Prison officers are not supposed to tell prisoners about other prisoners. I am a bit deaf and I can't catch what anyone is saying. The sound bounces off the concrete walls. Were they put up to it so their hostilities would force me to sign the bond? One of them to placate me says 'You should sign the bond and you can always break it'. I don't say anything except that she has a right to her opinion. It is freezing. The women huddle together like birds, to keep warm. After a bit we are told we can go inside to the association room, a room with a large TV, a table, a few chairs. The women sit on the table. Because there are not enough chairs I crouch on the floor. My problem is I can't hear what they are saying. They speak very fast with various Munster accents and the sing-song sound of Cork and the surrounding areas. There are fewer women here, only about ten. I don't understand the procedure but do catch on later. I find out that you don't have to spend all your allocated time outside: you can go back to your cell and be locked in if you want. So ends my first night.

In the morning the routine becomes clearer. I visit the Governor who says I can be free if I sign the bond or I can appeal if I want to. I get the feeling that he is embarrassed by my being there. I am supposed to have a hospital appointment to check my cancer. Leaving jail to go to hospital could attract the press. Prison governors are terrified of the press. I could go to Mountjoy Prison's Dóchas Centre in Dublin, but as my case in Ennis is still ongoing, it is more convenient to stay in Limerick so I can discuss my case with Ed Horgan, John Lannon and Zoe Lawlor who all live in Limerick.

On the question of the appeal he has a point. I am out on bail for my second charge, it would have been more sensible to have charged me with both offences after the second trial. The rules concerning the release of prisoners have changed. Before it was the governor who had authority, now it is the prison service.

Outside, Niall [Farrell, peace activist], by not going to jail, is able to work with Ed on publicising my imprisonment and flagging up my cancer. The big C terrifies everyone who doesn't understand the different types of cancer. But maybe I am near death's door, I don't know what the hospital says. Another supporter says I have Parkinson's disease because of my tremor. But in fact my tremor is caused by an old injury from the RUC in Belfast when they gave me a savage triple somersault, putting pressure on my neck. I know Shatter is getting deep into a mess in the Dáil and feel perhaps the Governor supports my stance.

I am told I am allowed two visits a week to prepare my case. Then onto another little cubbyhole, the officers have offices the size of rabbit hutches. I say that I didn't think I could remain in the cold for two hours, yes I need open air, but going round in circles for two hours is too long. The officer agrees and says I can come in when I want. Next the psychiatrist. A civilised man. He says Limerick is wrong for women as it was built and caters for men. He thinks of himself still as a radical and supports my stance. He tells me to keep a diary of everything that was going on.

The prison doctor has been there for 28 years and looks burnt-out. I later hear horrendous stories of the medical treatment women had received. I have a short interview with him where I speak about my cancer and my hospital appointment due in the middle of January. I say I do not want to be treated in Limerick as they would not know anything of my case.

The male prisoners cook and deliver the food to us. At dinner time when I am handed salad on the cardboard plate there is a message in biro written under it: 'Fair Play to you Missus Airport Woman!'

The organisation of my phone calls takes place in another little cubbyhole. The middle-aged officer seems to love sitting there, fascinated by the telephone calls to all over the world. I have my list. He phones each number to see if they will accept my call. If the phone is not answered it is taken off the list. The phone bills must be huge.

Rose

That afternoon my guardian angel peers over the slit in the door. Rose Lynch, Republican prisoner serving 12 and a half years, the only political prisoner here. She is a leading member of the Real IRA, who don't accept the Good Friday agreement and carry on the armed struggle. She shot a man called Patrick Darcy and her case received the tabloid treatment. It was all entangled with a feud in Dublin over the killing of one of the leaders of the Real IRA. There was some doubt if she in fact had been the gunwoman or she was taking the rap for others.

She's smiling. Rose always smiles. She's in her fifties, with a round angelic face and a soft Limerick accent. She runs the library, which is only a cupboard in the association room with a few shelves of books. She tells me there is going to be a demo outside the jail in support of me. She had been in the Dóchas Centre when Maura Harrington and Izzy Ní Ghraidm from the Rossport campaign were there. She says I should get permission from the Governor to visit her in her cell. I think that if she knows Irish she could help with the translation of Gabriel Rosenstock's Guantanamo poems from Irish into English.

Her cell is upstairs in the last part of the old jail, a single cell. The walls are completely covered with Republic pictures of demos, her father, her children and grandchildren. It is a cosy home for her. She is amazing. She organises the women's section and has brought in Red Cross classes. She tells me about what courses I can do and about the gym and music classes. She prefers Limerick because of the rigid timetables for locking in and out.

She is careful not to mix too much with the others. She rarely goes out to the yard and will only make brief appearances in the association room, for fear of being attacked. Many of the other prisoners also do not mix, preferring to stay in their cells only leaving for food or if they are going to a course.

Rose trained and practised as a community worker in Belfast. She has been a Republican since she was four. On her cell wall is a picture of a merry little blond girl waving a flag. She has a small coterie of women embroidering Republican handkerchiefs. We avoid talking politics.

She has no self-pity and knuckles under to serve her sentence. It could have been shortened if she had renounced the armed struggle and her role in the shooting. She had been studying community relations in the University of Cork; here she is taking an Open University degree in social management of traffic but has no internet to help her. She has a very good tutor and passed all her exams, the tabloids got hold of that and the headlines were dismissive of her. The tabloid papers do a lot of damage to prisoners. They are avidly read inside, particularly the local papers and headlines can create tension.

Rose keeps in touch with one of her daughters who is expecting a baby at any moment. Her daughter is pretty strong and is doing a five kilometre run every day to bring on the baby. Rose hopes the Governor will let her out to see the baby in hospital, even if she is handcuffed.

One day Rose comes into the association room with a tennis ball, throws it to one of the women and says: 'We never say anything nice about each other. Why don't you throw it to someone you like while saying why you like them?' The women quickly take to the game. I notice that a rather broody overweight woman is always with a really beautiful younger woman. She throws the ball to her saying 'I really like you', the younger woman blushes. I realise that Rose is right. The women here never express themselves as to why they like each other. Rose slips away after one round of the game.

I suggest to Rose that International Women's Day should be celebrated. I go to the Governor, who agrees. Rose swings into action and devises a programme for a week's celebrations. There will be poetry from Galway poet and playwright Rita Ann Higgins who gives poetry classes to the men, a karaoke evening, a quiz, a talent concert, a football match between the women and the prison officers and a lecture on drugs.

Rose unfortunately doesn't speak Gaelic, so I begin the translation of a Guantanamo poem by Shaker Aamer using a dictionary.

Fighting for the sake of peace

Peace they say
Spirit of peace
What kind of peace?
Seems they all talk, argue
All at loggerheads.
What kind of peace do they want?
What planning?
What causes the slaughter?
What is the reason?
It is not difficult to murder,
Arguments lead to slaughter.
They quarrel about peace.

www.shannonwatch.org

John Arden

Margaretta recalls an outing with her husband, John Arden, who was suffering with cancer. He was one of England's great writers, much neglected. His pioneering play about violence, Serjeant Musgrave's Dance, *premiered at the Royal Court Theatre in 1959, and was performed at Nottingham Playhouse in the 1970s.*

Thanks to a friend who had a car adapted for her mother, we were able to pay a final visit together to Shannon. John wanted to see two apple trees, which had been planted in memory of three activists and friends who had died: Emma Carroll; Liz Tully; and her partner Robin Hennessy. I wheeled John a short distance from our protest spot and there were the apple trees. On Liz's tree were beautiful ripe fruit. I plucked one and gave it to John who took a bite, looked at me and sang in his strong Yorkshire burr from the last speech of *Serjeant Musgrave's Dance*:

Your blood red rose is withered and gone
And fallen on the ground
And she who brought the apple down
Shall be my darling dear
For the apple holds a seed will grow
In live and lengthy joy
To raise a flourish tree of fruit
For ever and a day
With fal-la-la-the-dee, toor-a-ley
For ever and a day.

John died in March 2012 and an apple tree in his memory will be planted to join the other two at Shannon.

★ ★ ★

Gallows and Other Tales of Suspicion and Obsession, *by John Arden, is available from Spokesman.*

Michael Mears presents

COMRADES IN CONSCIENCE

An evening commemorating the courage of Britain's First World War conscientious objectors through drama, song and talks.

Speakers include:

CYRIL PEARCE and LOIS BIBBINGS

25 May 2016

CONWAY HALL

25 Red Lion Square, London WC1R 4RL (0207 405 1818)

Doors open 7pm for 7.30pm start (approx. finish 10pm)

Tickets £10 (£8 concessions) available at:

www.trybooking.co.uk/412 *or* www.conwayhall.org.uk

COMRADES IN CONSCIENCE

One hundred years to the day since general military conscription passed into law in Great Britain, the courageous men who resisted the compulsory call to arms, and the women who supported them, are remembered in an evening of differing perspectives – through drama, song, and talks.

THIS EVIL THING, by Michael Mears, is a dramatic overview of the conscientious objectors' struggle, and those instrumental in helping them - such as Bertrand Russell, Fenner Brockway and Catherine Marshall - which will be performed in a semi-staged reading by professional actors.

Speakers will include Cyril Pearce, author of *Comrades In Conscience*, about conscientious objectors in Huddersfield, and creator of the Pearce Register of British First World War COs, (now incorporated in the Imperial War Museum's online data platform 'Lives Of The First World War'); Professor Lois S. Bibbings, (University of Bristol), who has been researching and writing about WW1 COs since the 1990s, most notably in *Telling Tales About Men*; and Ben Copsey from the Peace Pledge Union.

Songs by Helen Chadwick Song Theatre will include a specially composed setting of the words found on the International COs memorial in Tavistock Square. There will also be a display of posters by Emily Johns, celebrating key figures and events from the First World War anti-war movement. This is a non-profit making evening, and any surplus will go to the Peace Pledge Union and Amnesty International.

25 May 2016

CONWAY HALL

25 Red Lion Square,
London WC1R 4RL
0207 405 1818

Tickets available at

www.trybooking.co.uk/412
or www.conwayhall.org.uk

A Pacifist Not at War

Michael Mears

Michael Mears is an actor and playwright who works predominantly in the theatre for companies such as the RSC and the National Theatre, as well as many regional theatres. His plays include the award-winning SOUP, about homelessness, and seven plays for BBC Radio 4.

'My dear mother and sister, I am now confined in a pit which started at the surface at three feet by two, and tapers off to two feet six inches by fifteen. Water was struck, but they continued digging until it was ten feet deep. The bottom is full of water, and I have to stand on two strips of wood all day long just above the waterline. There is no room to walk about and sitting is impossible. The sun beats down and through the long day there are only the walls of clay to look at …'

A letter written from someone languishing in Guantanamo Bay? Or in a cell in Saudi Arabia? No. This particular incarceration occurred at Cleethorpes on Humberside, one hundred years ago. The victim was James Brightmore, a solicitor's clerk from Manchester, and a conscientious objector.

When I read this, and other accounts of brutality inflicted by the British Army on those young British men whose consciences would not permit them to take part in the First World War, I felt moved, as an actor and playwright, to tell their story in some shape or form.

Thanks to a number of excellent books on the subject, including David Boulton's *Objection Overruled,* Jo Vellacott's *Bertrand Russell and the Pacifists,* (now reprinted by Spokesman under the title *Conscientious Objection*), John W. Graham's *Conscription and Conscience,* and more recently, Cyril Pearce's *Comrades In Conscience,* I was made aware of the extraordinary resistance that was put up to the introduction of military conscription, and the harsh challenges facing those men who refused to answer the summons to barracks. I learnt of the intricate network of helpers and supporters in places high and low, and the organisations that helped them in their struggle, pre-eminent amongst them, surely, the No-Conscription Fellowship, founded by Fenner Brockway in late 1914. And I was filled with admiration for the tireless efforts of those supporters, one of whom, of course, was Bertrand Russell.

In addition to his well-documented letters, articles and correspondence (see the excellent collection of his letters *A Pacifist At War,* edited by Nicholas Griffin), there is also Russell's *Autobiography.* While I found that the sections relating to the First World War paint a vivid overall picture of his journey through these enormous events, there were some incidents he touches on that left me hungry for more detail: tantalising glimpses of scenes which are not recorded or documented, but which cause a playwright to salivate at the prospect of what might have taken place.

For example, his description of bathing in the pond at Garsington, where he was staying at the house of his friends, the liberal MP Philip Morrell and his wife, Ottoline (lover and long-time friend and confidant of Russell) – then stepping out of the pond stark naked to find Henry Asquith on the bank. All Russell says is, 'The quality of dignity that should have characterized a meeting between the Prime Minister and a pacifist was somewhat lacking on this occasion.' A wonderfully droll comment, but what actually was said between them? I tried to imagine the subsequent discussion and possibly heated debate – hinting that it may have been Russell who planted in the PM's mind the idea of a 'conscience clause' to be included in the ominously imminent Military Service Act.

Many other heroes and heroines played their role in these epic events, too numerous to list here, but the remarkable Catherine Marshall must be mentioned, for her untiring, meticulous and ingenious work for the NCF. She became Russell's prime associate in the organisation as the war progressed. Another is Clifford Allen, the agnostic socialist and quietly charismatic chairman of the NCF, who Russell replaced when it became Allen's turn to be arrested for refusing to report to barracks. And, of course, the 16,000 plus COs, who endured endless indignities, contempt and harsh treatment at the hands of the military.

Some accounts of COs being grilled and investigated by their Local Tribunals, to assess whether their conscientious objection was genuine and whether therefore they might be exempted from military service, would provoke laughter and derision, were they not true. An 18 year old CO denied exemption because he was considered too young to have a conscience; a declared atheist told he couldn't *possibly* have a conscience; a CO who was a piano tuner by trade denied exemption because how could he know what use the pianos he tuned might be put to? They might be used to play patriotic songs or military marches, so how could he possibly claim to be a conscientious objector? And so it went on.

Arrests followed, COs were forcibly escorted to barracks, orders given to put on uniform, do drill, carry out other tasks, all of which, politely refused, would result in punishments, bread and water diets, solitary confinement, or worse – such as entombment in a ten foot deep pit, as James Brightmore was, on the pretext that no cell was available for him. Another CO, Jack Gray, was subjected to a regime of cruelty culminating in a rope tied around his stomach and being pushed into a pond eight or nine times, and dragged out each time by the rope. The pond contained sewage.

At least COs couldn't face the ultimate threat – execution – as they were not in the war zone, and therefore not deemed to be on active service. Until, that is, the Army began sending them across to France, which meant they now found themselves in the most precarious situation: 35 COs in particular, who were hauled before a Field General Court Martial – the maximum penalty, if found guilty, was death.

And here there is another intriguing glimpse in Russell's *Autobiography* of an unrecorded scene – a deputation to Downing Street to avert this crisis, to inform the Prime Minister what the Army was up to, seemingly without the government's knowledge or approval. Russell says, 'Although he [Asquith] was just starting for Dublin, he listened to us courteously, and took the necessary action.' Again, it was tempting as a playwright to try and flesh out this scene – Russell biding his time, perhaps, while Catherine Marshall spoke, or Philip Snowden, the Independent Labour Party MP – until Russell could hold off no longer, perhaps erupting in a passionate appeal to the Prime Minister: 'The point is will they be shot? Because if these COs are executed, simply because their consciences would not permit them to take up arms against a fellow human being, it will be the greatest stain imaginable on our nation's reputation!'

The 35 were indeed sentenced to death, but had their sentences commuted to ten years penal servitude in a civil prison back in England. Surely Russell's role in this outcome cannot be denied? In time they were joined by Russell himself who, in 1918, was sentenced by a somewhat vindictive judge to six months in Brixton Prison – on account of one mildly provocative sentence in an article he'd written, about the likelihood of American soldiers being used in this country as strike-breakers.

When the Armistice finally came, Russell was out of prison, observing the revelling crowds in the Tottenham Court Road. As he says in his *Autobiography*:

'I felt strangely solitary amid the rejoicings, like a ghost dropped by accident from another planet. True, I rejoiced also, but I could find nothing in common between my rejoicing and that of the crowd.'

More than 16,500 young men refused to act against their consciences. 31 of those lost their sanity, and 73 died due to illness or mistreatment while in the hands of the military. It's a tiny number compared to the 19,240 British soldiers who lost their lives on the first day of the Battle of the Somme. But with so much emphasis during these anniversary years on the men who fought in the trenches, there is a pressing need for the other side of the story to be told, for it to be repeatedly told, to redress the balance: the story of the young men who showed a different kind of courage, *refusing* to fight, whatever punishments were thrown at them, passionately believing that this was the best, indeed the only way to truly serve the cause of peace.

Russell was a pacifist at war; I am a pacifist *not* at war – someone who hasn't had his pacifism truly tested. And the question that has been haunting me is this: how would I have responded if I'd been a young man in 1914? Would I have had the courage to endure the bullying, the abuse, the solitary confinement, the imprisonment in a ten-foot deep pit, the very real threat of execution? I fervently hope that I would have had the courage – but there's no way of knowing, is there?

At Conway Hall, London, at 7.30pm on 25 May 2016, one hundred years since the very day that military conscription was extended to include married men aged 18 to 41, we will commemorate and celebrate the courage of these COs through drama, song, and with talks by Cyril Pearce, Lois S. Bibbings (author of Telling Tales About Men), *and Ben Copsey from the Peace Pledge Union. Please join us if you can.*

Violence of the 'lambs'

Tony Simpson

On the 150th anniversary, we revisit Nottingham's by-election of 1866 which brought Bertrand Russell's parents to the city.

By-election fever gripped Nottingham during spring 1866. The General Election result of the preceding year was put aside and Mr Speaker issued a New Writ

'for the electing of two Burgesses to serve in this present Parliament for the Town and County of the Town of Nottingham, in the room of Sir Robert Juckes Clifton, baronet, and Samuel Morley, Esq., whose elections have been determined to be void.'

A Parliamentary inquiry had heard telling evidence of bribery and systematic disruption of opponents' campaigns by Sir Robert, whose statue stands alone to this day, gazing eastwards by the Toll Bridge over River Trent as it slides past Nottingham, dividing England's North from South. Is Sir Robert looking for his 'lambs'?

Sir Robert Clifton by Wilford Toll Bridge

As *The Times* reported (26.3.1866), the evidence was almost solely confined to accounts 'by the roughs or "lambs" ' of the part they took in the disturbances prior to and at the election:

> 'John Terry, tinman and brazier, was recalled and examined at considerable length. He stated that the mob broke into Paget and Morley's committee-room, in St. Ann's Ward, and completely gutted it. Witness was here shown two photographs, which he said were accurate representations of the committee room before and after the attack. After the hacking, the "lambs" retired to the Butchers' Arms, and refreshed themselves with something to drink. Witness went with half-a-dozen of them to the Assembly Rooms for payment, and saw several gentlemen, one of whom paid him £28, which was to be divided among the roughs.'

'Gutted' appears an accurate description:

Liberal committee rooms after riot, Nottingham, 1865
Copyright: Nottingham City Council

Who would be the by-election candidates for the Liberal Party this time? Step forward, somewhat reluctantly, John Russell, Viscount Amberley. Amberley, as he was known, had been defeated at Leeds in the General Election of 1865, but had given a good account of himself, particularly in relation to 'Reform', the burning issue of the day. Reform meant extending the suffrage, or vote, to many more men (not to women, although Lady Kate Amberley soon advocated such), but it was proposed that this be on the basis of property ownership or rent paid above a certain level, in order to exclude the burgeoning working class.

Lord John Russell, Amberley's father, was the architect of the Reform

Act of 1832 which, in fact, made only a limited extension of the franchise to small landowners, tenant farmers, shopkeepers, and householders paying a yearly rental of £10 or more. Many others were excluded. The Act also redistributed seats to the growing cities from the countryside, described by one Tory MP as 'Russell's Purge'.

In Nottingham feelings about Parliamentary Reform ran high, as Kate Amberley later indicated, when she went to see the Castle 'burned down in 1831 because the Duke of Newcastle, its proprietor, voted against the Reform Bill'.

The 1832 Act, significant though it was, excluded many men and all women from voting for their Member of Parliament. Indeed, it was not until 1928 and the Equal Franchise Act that women over 21 were able to vote, and finally obtained the same voting rights as men. In the 1830s, millions of excluded people campaigned and clamoured for the right to the vote. Industrialising cities such as Nottingham saw their populations increase rapidly with the arrival of new workers from rural areas and further afield, from Ireland, to work in the growing lace, hosiery and related textile trades. Conditions were dire, at work and at home, as more and more people crammed into Broadmarsh, Narrowmarsh and other central areas of the city. In these grim circumstances, Nottingham became a major centre of Chartist agitation and activity.

The Charter's demands included that all men have the vote in secret ballots; that Members of Parliament should be paid, and that the property qualification to become an MP should be abolished; and that there be annual elections in constituencies of equal size. Chartism's extra-Parliamentary struggle focused on fundamental reform of the Westminster Parliament, attracting the support of millions of people, particularly from the disenfranchised working class in Nottingham and elsewhere. So it was that Feargus O'Connor, leading Chartist and land reformer from County Cork in Ireland, was elected in Nottingham in 1847 as the country's first and only Chartist MP. A year later, he presided over the last great Chartist demonstration in London, after which the movement declined, although the objectives for which it campaigned remained live. O'Connor's statue, 'erected by his admirers' in 1859, now stands in a quiet and leafy corner of Nottingham's Arboretum.

It was against this background of long-term agitation for more people to have the vote that, in 1865, Lord John Russell became Prime Minister for a second time, succeeding Palmerston, who had died. Russell was much more Reform-minded than Palmerston, and he prepared a second Reform bill. Amberley, his 23-year-old eldest son, supported his father in this cause, and sought a career in politics. So it was that the Liberal committee in Nottingham lobbied Amberley to stand as one of their two candidates in the by-election for the dual-member parliamentary borough. But Nottingham's reputation for rough politics preceded it. Initially, the Prime Minister was very reluctant, but later told his son:

'*I have been reading the proceedings at Nottingham, and I think that if there is a good requisition, and a fair prospect of a quiet election, you might accept their invitation. But not if a fellow like Sir R Clifton is to stand on the Conservative side, and bring a mob of ruffians at his heels. The respectable people of the town might secure you, if they chose, against such outrages.*'

Lord John Russell

Kate Amberley

Viscount Amberley

So it was that Amberley, Kate and Mr Cossham, the other Liberal candidate, set out by train to Nottingham on Monday 30 April, 11 days before the poll. First impressions did not encourage the young couple, as Kate wrote in her journal:

'... *We arrived at Nottingham station at 5.55 and were met by Mr Richards and about 40 others. We got into an open carriage with a postilion in blue and drove to our Inn 'The Flying Horse', the old liberal headquarters – an old fashioned rambling inn, Miss Malpas the landlady. We had a sitting room a very low one with 5 windows, so that we could see up and down the street from one on to the market place. We had tea and went to the liberal electors meeting in the Exchange. Before we went all the Committee (150 in number) came to the Flying Horse to be introduced to Amberley and to go with him to the Exchange. There were propositions to take me in to the building a back way to avoid any people, but I was determined to go with Amberley and so I did. We walked together, 2 rows of 6 men arm in arm in front of us as a sort of guard for us, and the same behind; as we went through the street, there were groans and hisses and cheers.*

Once inside the building they made way for us and we got easily on to the platform where I sat on the right of the Chairman and we were much cheered. Dr Ransome was in the chair. Amberley spoke very well indeed, very slowly and distinctly but I fear his voice did not go to the end of the hall. I liked the speech very much indeed. Mr Cossham's which was earnest and fluent was very much inferior in style and tone.

They cheered me very much. Coming away, I took A's arm and Mr Cossham's; at the door we found a body of police who surrounded us, and our own people also, and we went out so into the mob, who groaned and hissed and cheered and tried to break through the police and there was a regular scuffle and tumble and people knocked about but I stuck fast to Amberley and did not mind at all; with some difficulty a way was made for us to get into our own door and then we went up stairs and showed ourselves at the window and were cheered and hooted.

Several people came up to us, and told us that was quiet for Nottingham and that we must expect it to get much warmer as time went on. Amberley did not much like it, or the prospect of any roughness, and said he had been assured it would be a quiet election. We went to bed very sorry we had ever come here.'

Tuesday brought news that an experienced former MP, Bernal Osborne, might join the fight and split the Liberal vote. He duly arrived the next day, altering the electoral arithmetic. Kate confided to her journal that there were 'troops in the town now, for fear of riot at this election'. She continued:

'The liberal party all seem in a state as BO held his meeting with Sir Robert Clifton in the chair and declared his intention of standing. They say it is impossible now to calculate chances and see how votes will split and that BO will unite with Jenkinson (the Tory candidate) and so may win. Also unlimited money is to be spent on the Tory side, which will render it a very unpleasant contest, in nature just like the last and just such a one as Amberley dislikes, so he says he will retire unless BO does.'

Political calculations in London proceeded in another direction. Lady Russell offered the young Amberley family the use of Downing Street as a home during the current session of Parliament, 'which we liked very much', wrote Kate. This prime offer encouraged an aspiring politician and his young wife. Intriguingly, the Prime Minister 'rather wished Bernal Osborne to come in,' Kate added.

On Friday, Kate found time to visit Mundella's factory for new stockings. After the weekend's campaigning, in Monday evening sunshine, she and her husband walked through the Market Place to the Committee Rooms. Another candidate, Falkener, was speaking in the Market Place and 'many people came from him to groan at us, but presently a crowd assembled round us cheering, and quite drowned the groans'. The Market Place was crowded that evening as Bernal Osborne also had a meeting at the same time, with Sir Robert Clifton again presiding.

Wednesday was Nomination Day and the Amberleys were far from confident of their prospects. Kate wrote:

' We left the Flying Horse at 9.30 with our Committee and several ladies and went to the Exchange the long way and through a crowd that groaned and cheered all the way enthusiastically ... I had on my orange shawl and bonnet; and Lady and Miss Jenkinson were in blue on the opposite side of the Meetings. The crowd was wonderfully quiet for Nottingham ... Tin plates were waved about in the crowd in derision of S G Jenkinson's plate, which he is said to boast of. Also a baby doll was held up to Amberley, a bear and traitor for B Osborne, and a bottle of water for Cossham. It was a grand sight; the market place was full half way and tightly packed. The show of hands was greatly in favour of BO and Sir G Jenkinson. A and Cossham seemed to have a very small minority ... '

Polling Day, Thursday 10 May, dawned fine and bright. Kate watched the Central Committee Rooms from her window in the Flying Horse, and heard the cheering whenever announcements were put up. Later in the day, she and Amberley toured the Ward Committees in a carriage. By her account, they were

'much cheered at each but received with lots of boohs and shouts of derision in the streets mixed with cries of cow-juice, pump-handle, Baby, etc and faces and jeers. As we returned across the Market Place which was crowded, the mob rushed towards us and surrounded the carriage. When we got in I went to the window to show myself and had a stick thrown at me, also some dirt that hit me on the eye. There was a great mob in the street and they fisticuffed a good deal amongst one another and attacked one woman because she had yellow ribbons in her hair ...

A and I stayed in together and the accounts of the poll kept getting worse and worse; Osborne was above Amberley at 3 and Jenkinson so near and we heard so much bribery going on, that Amberley gave up all hope and was very low about it ... At 4 a woman at the window told me Osborne and Amberley were in but we did not believe her as the returns could not be known yet, then came in a maid of the house and told us we had got in ...

Amberley went off to the Committee Rooms balcony to thank the people and came back on foot, through a hooting mob ... The Mayor called on us with his wife and may other people. Amberley was much pleased and I was for him. I am very glad he has not had the contest for nothing. Cossham is very sorry, and so are his party ...'

Bernal Osborne beat Cossham to the second seat, so the Prime Minister, Lord John Russell, got his preferred ticket. Friday was the Declaration of Poll and Amberley and Kate went to be photographed at Cox, St James' Street. They were done together 'standing up'. A few weeks later, in June 1866, Lord John Russell's second reform bill was defeated by dissident Liberals and he resigned as Prime Minister. Amberley continued as Member of Parliament for Nottingham until the general election of November 1868, when he flitted, unsuccessfully, to stand in Devon. Meanwhile, Disraeli's Second Reform Act of 1867 had doubled the size of the electorate, who duly showed their gratitude by defeating the Tory Party at the 1868 election. Notwithstanding the new Act, many men and all women were still denied their vote. And corrupt elections endure to this day.

Bertrand Russell, born in 1872, was the youngest son of Kate and John Amberley.

Goat

Don't fall for it – the sidelong look, that punted puck
of a pupil - Goat wants nothing more

than to slip a cleated mitt beneath a fuss of skirts,
raise merry hell.
                Button up. Keep very still.

Don't think about that knock-kneed hopscotch,
dapper, quickstepped, keen. The long, tall grin.

Goat means to take your shoulder as a bit
between his teeth, skip in and out like nifty ribbonwork.

Call him *Stickpin*. Call him *Sheershank*.
Don't call to him at all –   *But oh, my girl, you will.*

Call it fancy. Call it whim.
Call it a door opening on the slant stair

to the room you didn't know was there,
        though you've lived here all your life –

        And come down with the dawn.
Now you've been gone too long -

the dance was over weeks ago, your guests
have all gone home.
        Now you're shoeless, skint

and swindled. Now the daybreak wants to know.
Now the piper's piping up beyond the *gate* -   *too late, my girl, too late.*

                Abigail Parry

Abigail Parry visited The Spokesman and kindly offered some poems. She is poet in residence at the National Videogame Arcade, Nottingham, and recently won the Ballymaloe International Poetry Prize in association with The Moth arts and literature journal, published in County Cavan, Ireland.

Submerged politics of UK nuclear power

Is Trident renewal influencing UK energy policy?

Phil Johnstone
Andy Stirling

Philip Johnstone is Research Fellow, Science Policy Research Unit, University of Sussex. Andy Stirling is Professor of Science & Technology Policy, SPRU, and co-director of the ESRC STEPS Centre, University of Sussex.

With Parliament now getting ready to vote on the 'main gate' decision on renewal of the Trident programme, 2016 is set to be a decisive year for the future of UK nuclear weapons capabilities. Political opposition has grown in Parliament, with both the Scottish National Party (SNP) and Labour leaderships now opposed to Trident renewal. At a lifetime cost variously estimated between £31 Billion[1] and over £100 billion[2], the political and economic stakes are very high. Debate is becoming increasingly heated over the practicalities, costs, ethical and strategic implications. Many of these arguments are covered extensively elsewhere, and are not repeated here.[2-6]

Instead, this article looks at another possible implication of Trident renewal which has remained almost completely 'under the radar' of contemporary policy and academic debate. This concerns the recent history of the UK civil nuclear power industry, which also involves remarkably similar stories of delays, cost overruns, questions of necessity and performance, and critical comparisons with strategies in other countries and arguments for superior alternatives.[7]

The intensity of UK commitments to civil nuclear power is also looking increasingly anomalous on the world stage. The contrast with Germany is especially striking, with the UK hosting a massively less successful nuclear engineering and power industry and enjoying a renewable resource that is the envy of Europe.[8] Yet it is Germany (with a track record of prescience in past industrial policy decisions), that is undertaking a complete nuclear phase-out by 2022, whilst the UK Government doggedly pursues a 'nuclear renaissance'. In a current academic research project now nearing completion[9], we are systematically exploring possible reasons for the UK's internationally-anomalous commitment to nuclear energy. And this is where there emerges a seeming connection to Trident.

Of course, concerns over climate change and energy security certainly play a part in UK interest in nuclear power. But they do not explain why the UK should be so unusually intense in its nuclear enthusiasm. As in Germany, such reasons might speak even more strongly for alternative policies. In our research, we have (like others) examined in great detail, issues of energy economics, industrial policy, available resources, security of supply, political lobbies, the history of energy institutions, technological lock-in, and different aspects and qualities of democratic decision making.[8] Although the issues are highly complex and any full explanation must be multi-causal, it is difficult to avoid recognising that there emerges a further factor – one which is all the more important to address, because it has hitherto escaped virtually any attention whatsoever.

In short, these neglected questions concern the extent to which UK policy commitments to nuclear power reflect a deeper perceived imperative to maintain national capabilities to design, build, operate, staff, regulate and decommission nuclear propelled submarines. Without nuclear propulsion, submarines would not, in current military opinion, display the requisite endurance, stealth, speed and robustness to serve as credible platforms or guardians of strategic nuclear capabilities.[10] In influential quarters, capabilities to maintain naval nuclear propulsion is thus seen to constitute a serious bottleneck in the sustaining of crucial wider strategic military capabilities. And these are in turn of crucial importance to a particular UK identity as an 'outsized power' that 'punches above its weight'.[11]

The challenge is that nuclear submarines are among the most complex and demanding of human artefacts. In a time of serous decline in UK manufacturing capacities, maintaining this capability places especially serious demands.[12,13] The security sensitivities preclude much of the kind of national outsourcing that is so routine in other industries. So, the ability of the UK to maintain a cherished elite identity on the world stage, rest on its ability to find as many alternative ways as possible to secure the national reservoirs of highly specialist expertise, education, training, skills, production and regulation necessary to sustain nuclear submarines. In order to achieve this, however, it is not essential that the UK take a lead in building civilian nuclear power reactors. All that is required is that crucial parts of the submarine industry secure key places in civilian nuclear power supply chains.

If this is a factor in the peculiar intensity of UK government commitments to civil nuclear power, then what is most remarkable is that it remains entirely unacknowledged in any policy literature that we are aware of concerning the formal rationales for a UK 'nuclear renaissance'. It would perhaps be in the nature of such a sensitive imperative, that the Government might be expected to be discrete about it. Yet we believe we have found strong circumstantial evidence, that this actually forms a crucial general pressure that has operated decisively at important critical junctures in UK nuclear policy making. It is this evidence that the rest of this article examines.

A military nuclear connection, in this day and age?

It is for good reason that something of a taboo has arisen over the years around emphasising any kind of linkage between civilian and military-related nuclear issues. The topic is the object of much misleading casual comment. Albeit not perfect, strict safeguards have been in place for decades to prevent cross-overs in usage of fissile materials and ensure that civilian nuclear power does not compound risks of nuclear weapons proliferation.[14] Dedicated institutions like the International Atomic Energy Agency (IAEA) and Euratom work strongly to ensure the separation of civilian and military related nuclear matters and uphold the Nuclear Non-Proliferation Treaty.

Perhaps even more significantly, the reduction in strategic arsenals following the end of the Cold War means that key nuclear weapons materials such as plutonium are actually in surplus on the military side.[15] The situation is arguably a little more complex and obscure with regard to other specialist materials such as tritium[16], but with many other possibilities in play, this also seems largely irrelevant to any pressure to maintain a large indigenous civil nuclear power industry. So, although the history of nuclear power in the UK (as elsewhere) is inextricably tied to ambitions around nuclear weapons[17,18] – and the connection remains relevant around horizontal proliferation – it is not credible to argue that nuclear weapons materials production might currently constitute a significant driver of UK civil nuclear policies.

But this is not a story concerning fissile materials. Nor is it about the design or manufacture of vital missile or warhead components, many of which are supplied by the United States.[3,4] Indeed the issue here is not about nuclear weapons at all, but about the ability to construct and operate the submarine platforms on which their effective strategic performance is seen to depend. And – although also linked in many ways to US designs and supply chains – it is an ability to maintain minimal independent national capabilities to build and operate these nuclear-propelled Trident submarines (and associated attack boats) that remains the focus of an intense and rather anxious national debate on the military side.

Here, a long series of government reports, consultancy studies, select committee inquiries, lobby documents and dedicated new institutions all indicate, very strongly, the weight of priority attached to maintaining a threatened national capability. All that is missing, is any clear policy acknowledgement that it is this perceived imperative that is exerting an influence on the strength of commitment to maintaining a UK supply chain sustained by a civilian nuclear power programme. But we think we have found some illuminating tell-tale signs of such links.

The intensity of the UK's commitment to civilian nuclear power is puzzling

Before turning to these, it is important to substantiate quite how distinctive are the current levels of UK Government support for nuclear power. With Energy Minister Amber Rudd recently stating that '[i]*nvesting in nuclear is what this Government is all about for the next twenty years*'[19], the UK is the main governmental advocate on the world stage of a 'nuclear renaissance'. A few countries have larger envisaged programmes in absolute terms[20] (most also, incidentally, operators of nuclear submarines). But these nuclear programmes are much smaller in relative terms when compared with plans in the same countries to exploit low carbon renewable energy options. Globally, investments in renewable electricity generating capacity exceed even that for all fossil fuels put together, leaving nuclear far behind.[21]

Yet UK Government support for a 'nuclear renaissance' remains larger than (and in large part an *alternative* to) efforts to develop its own especially attractive national renewable resources.[22] And what is especially striking here, is how persistent these enthusiasms have remained for a 'nuclear renaissance', despite repeated serious set-backs. The detailed ways in which the UK will deliver on this emphatic commitment are amazingly volatile. Since 2006, a series of radically different designs have each been confidently identified before being abandoned, including designs from US-Japanese, Chinese and French-led consortia – and now, most recently, an as-yet entirely undeveloped US/UK concept for a new small modular reactor.[23]

Nor does past UK history in the nuclear sector offer any encouragement for such an optimistic attitude. Following a series of earlier policy disasters, recent further blows include the withdrawal of multiple earlier prospective reactor constructors[24], massive over-runs in time and cost for similar planned reactors[25], the impossibility of securing private finance[26], the imposing of punishing terms by the current Chinese government financial backers[27], the revelation of a catastrophic defect in a key reactor component[28], and the presently-threatened bankruptcy or withdrawal of the only serious current contender for actually constructing the next UK nuclear plant.[29]

All this has occurred against the backdrop of ample evidence for the ready availability of more cost-effective zero-carbon resources for electricity generation in the UK. Under the same presently-envisaged contracts that are currently evidently viewed as insufficient by the prospective developers of the Hinkley Point C plant, EDF, British electricity consumers will be locked into funding this plant with guaranteed prices over 35 years that are almost three times the current wholesale price of electricity.[30]

The 'strike price' of £92.50/KWh agreed 'behind closed doors' with EDF is significantly higher than the government's own figures for comparable contracts for renewable electricity.[31] And worldwide statistics show unequivocally that nuclear costs continue to rise, whilst global renewable energy costs are falling. National industrial, employment and investment opportunities presented by capital-intensive renewable energy infrastructures are at least equal to those offered by nuclear power. Operational challenges posed by particular renewable technologies such as wind, which are intermittent in their output, are not trivial. But these do not arise until system penetrations that are much greater than presently envisaged scales of development. And they are, anyhow, balanced by a series of countervailing qualities in distributed electricity technologies that are actually seen in countries such as Germany and Denmark as advantages when compared with inflexible centralised 'base load' nuclear power.[32]

Of course, much scope remains for argument on all sides. Energy issues are complex, uncertain and ambiguous. But it is not necessary to be an unqualified critic of nuclear power, to appreciate that it is extraordinarily difficult to reconcile the intensity of UK government commitments to nuclear power with the recent history of experience in this field, neither with established global trends, nor with the manifest cost-effectiveness and availability of low carbon alternatives. Against a backdrop of a stronger national nuclear industry and a weaker national renewable resource,

Germany presents an especially telling contrast. At the very least, it does seem that some other explanation is required for why the UK should remain so internationally distinctive in the intensity of its attachment to a 'nuclear renaissance'.

The 2003 Energy White paper: an exception that proves the rule?
In seeking to understand the causes of this evidently peculiar form of technological lock-in, it is illuminating to consider a brief period when the attachment was briefly broken. After a series of policy catastrophes driven by successive episodes of apparent UK Government credulity in the face of over-optimistic representations of nuclear interests[33-35], the 1997 election saw all political parties, if reluctantly, accepting that nuclear power had become uncompetitive and unattractive compared with alternatives.[36] In the ensuing new enthusiasm for public participation in the early years of Tony Blair's New Labour administration, an unprecedented move occurred when the Cabinet Office initiated an important review of energy policy that was not primarily written by Government civil servants but also included crucial inputs from independent energy experts.[37] Also relevant is that this arrived at its energy focus through a rather convoluted route that began as a review of resources, quickly evolving to include renewable resources, and then expanding to address other energy options more generally. In this way the energy issue was approached 'under the radar', by-passing the 'usual suspects' in established ministries concerned with nuclear strategies.

For whatever reason, the resulting report became the most detailed UK government analysis to date of the imperatives involved in undertaking a transition to low carbon energy systems. Following up on this, the Energy White Paper of 2003 concluded, in an exceptional historic moment, that nuclear power was not an attractive option – and that a shift towards a more decentralised energy system based around renewables and energy efficiency would be preferable.[38]

What followed was one of the most remarkable turnarounds in recent UK policy-making on any issue – offering some of the most compelling circumstantial evidence for the relevance of military submarine capabilities as a driver of civil nuclear policy. In an unprecedented short period after the publication of the 2003 Energy White Paper, Tony Blair announced in 2005 a completely new energy review. Without providing any substantive reason as to its necessity, this further energy review was undertaken by a small group of civil servants in the Cabinet Office. According to one nuclear proponent, Simon Taylor, this involved a select group that most civil servants in the Cabinet Office did not even know existed, working 'in secret' specifically to re-examine the case for nuclear power.[39]

The resulting energy review was thus far shorter than the earlier process, entirely dependent on narrow government specialists, and largely conducted in secret. The consultation for this review was managed by AEA Technology (the former Atomic Energy Authority). Amidst widespread bewilderment and criticism of this superficial process was a finding by the Royal Courts of Justice that the new government consultation was actually 'unlawful' in its bias towards nuclear power.[40] Although by no means opposed to nuclear power, the House of Commons Trade and Industry Select Committee also concluded that the consultation was a 'rubber stamping' exercise to reverse the conclusions of the more rigorous, longer, and independent energy review of 2002-3 and construct an apparent 'need' for new nuclear build.[41] Tellingly, Tony Blair's response to this formidable reaction was that it 'would not affect policy at all'.[42] A second rapid consultation was staged, abandoned by non-governmental organisations as again being flawed[43], and by 2008 a final new nuclear White Paper was released with exactly the same conclusions.[44]

With the rationale for this remarkable turnaround so manifestly determined in such authoritative ways as inadequate, what evidence might there be for alternative explanations? And it is here that our story turns to the apparent links with military submarine capabilities.

Submerged factors influencing UK energy policy?

It was in exactly this 'critical juncture' between 2003 and 2006, that an unprecedented intensification can be seen in policy activities around UK 'submarine nuclear capabilities'. Much of this discussion is internal to the military sector and addresses civil nuclear policy only incidentally. But the overall picture is very clear – it was at precisely the point when civil nuclear power fell out of official favour that anxieties arose in an unprecedented and abrupt fashion that a serious threat had arisen to the ability of the UK to maintain a national capability to build and operate nuclear submarines.

One significant element in this wider series of developments was an extremely energetic and well-targeted initiative by interests associated with the Barrow Shipyard where all UK submarines are constructed – formerly by Vickers and now by BAE Systems. Formed in March 2004, this well-funded group, Keep Our Future Afloat (KOFAC), involved trade unions, local councils, and county councils in concerted efforts to sustain the construction of nuclear powered submarines at the Barrow shipyard.[45]

Targeting politicians and party conferences, producing key reports and submitting evidence to both civilian energy policy reviews and defence reviews, the intense lobbying campaign came to be seen by parliamentarians as 'one of the most effective' that they had ever encountered.[45]

There emerged during this same 'critical juncture' defined by the unprecedented turnaround in civil nuclear energy policy a series of other remarkable indications of the political energy unleashed by concerns over submarine nuclear capabilities. It was in 2005 that the Ministry of Defence funded the RAND Corporation to conduct an in-depth three volume study of the 'nuclear submarine industrial base'.[46-48] Concerns were explicitly discussed over whether the UK would have the key relevant skills to construct nuclear submarines.[49] There ensued a series of Select Committee inquiries into exactly this topic.[10] Evidence was heard from a wide range of interested parties, many of whom explicitly addressed the relevance to the maintaining of UK nuclear submarine capabilities of the parallel sustaining of a healthy civil nuclear industry.

Other reports on exactly this theme were also produced around this time by other bodies including the International Institute for Strategic Studies[50], and the Royal United Services Institute.[51] The latter was led by a senior figure from inside BAE Systems who – among other interesting allusions to linkages between civil and military industries – referred to strategies in other cases under which particular military programmes can be 'masked' in other activities. It was on this basis that the founding moves were made behind major current policy initiatives with missions spanning both military and civilian sectors. The Cogent Programme[52], Key Suppliers Forum[53] and Nuclear Institute[54], for instance, all have explicit responsibilities to protect capabilities relevant to both military and civilian nuclear sectors.

Taken together – and despite the lack of explicit policy acknowledgements – the evidence seems clear. As observed by Oxford Economics in a detailed recent report for the UK Government on the UK nuclear supply chain:

> 'The naval and civil reactor industries are often viewed as separate and to some extent unrelated from a government policy perspective. However, the timeline of the UK nuclear industry has clear interactions between the two, particularly from a supply chain development point of view.'[55]

So, important as it is, the debate over Trident may not be all that it seems. If this analysis is even partly correct, the stakes are even more extensive than the momentous issues that at first meet the eye. Bound up with the grave ethical, strategic, economic and political concerns that bear directly on the renewal of nuclear weapons capabilities, are a series of further evident questions around deeper forms of lock-in to nuclear technologies more generally. That these questions remain largely undiscussed in UK policy debates over either Trident or nuclear power, arguably constitutes one of the gravest implications of all – one that threatens not just the outcomes of policy making in either of these particular areas, but the very processes of democracy itself.

Notes

1 HM Government. National Security Strategy and Strategic Defence and Security Review 2015. London: The Stationary Office, Crown Copyright; 2015.
2 CND. People not Trident: the economic case against Trident. London: Campaign for Nuclear Disarmament; 2014.
3 Edwards R. Revealed: MoD's new multi-million pound Trident deal with America. The Herald Scotland online [Internet]. Edinburgh; 2014 Nov 23; Available from: http://www.heraldscotland.com/news/home-news/revealed-mods-new-multi-million-pound-trident-deal-with-america.25941179
4 Ritchie N. A nuclear weapons free world? Britain, Trident, and the challenges ahead. London: Palgrave Macmillan; 2012.
5 BASIC. Trident Replacement : The Facts. :1–6. 2013.
6 BASIC. US-UK Mutual Defence Agreement Renewal 2014: a foregone conclusion? [Internet]. British American Security Information Council Webpages. 2014 [cited 2016 Apr 24]. Available from: http://www.basicint.org/blogs/2014/02/us-uk-mutual-defence-agreement-renewal-2014-foregone-conclusion
7 Johnstone P, Stirling A. Why Germany is dumping nuclear power – and Britain isn't [Internet]. The Conversation. 2015 [cited 2016 Apr 23]. Available from: https://theconversation.com/why-germany-is-dumping-nuclear-power-and-britain-isnt-46359
8 Johnstone P, Stirling A. Comparing Nuclear Power Trajectories in Germany And the UK : From 'Regimes' to 'Democracies' in Sociotechnical Transitions and Discontinuities. SPRU Work Pap Ser [Internet]. 2015;18:1–86. Available from: www.sussex.ac.uk
9 SPRU. Governance of Discontinuity in Technological Systems (DiscGo) [Internet]. Science Policy Research Unit (SPRU), University of Sussex webpages. 2016 [cited 2016 Apr 27]. Available from: http://www.sussex.ac.uk/sussexenergygroup/research/current/discgo
10 House of Commons Defence Committee. The Defence Industrial Strategy: update. London: The Stationary Office; 2007.
11 The Herald. UK needs Trident to maintain 'outsized role on global stage', says

US. The Scottish Herald [Internet]. Edinburgh; 2016 Feb; Available from: http://www.heraldscotland.com/news/14275047.UK_needs_Trident_to_maint ain_outsized_role_on_global_stage___says_US/?ref=rss

12 Ireland G. The Challenges Facing the UK Submarine Base. Vol. 3. London; 2012.
13 Edwards R. MoD struggling with shortage of nuclear engineers [Internet]. The Herald Scotland online. 2015 [cited 2015 Mar 8]. Available from: http://www.heraldscotland.com/news/home-news/mod-struggling-with-shortage-of-nuclear-engineers.120130614
14 IAEA. IAEA Safeguards in Practice [Internet]. International Atomic Energy Agency Webpages. 2016 [cited 2016 Apr 27]. Available from: https://www.iaea.org/safeguards/safeguards-in-practice
15 IPFM. 2015 Fissile Materials Report: Nuclear Weapon and Fissile Material Stockpiles and Production. INternational Panel on Fissile Materials; 2015.
16 Bergeron K. Tritium on ice: The dangerous new alliance of nuclear weapons and nuclear power. Boston: MIT Press; 2002.
17 Arnold L. Britain and the H-Bomb. Basingstoke: Palgrave; 2001.
18 Sovacool BK, Valentine S V. The International Politics of Nuclear Power: Economics, Security, and Governance. Oxon: Routledge; 2012.
19 BBC Radio 4. The Today programme interview with Amber Rudd. UK: BBC; 2016.
20 Schneider M, Froggatt A. World nuclear industry status report 2015. Paris: A Mycle Schneider Consulting Project; 2015.
21 Randall T. Fossil fuels just lost the race against renewables [Internet]. Bloomberg. 2015 [cited 2016 Apr 21]. Available from: http://www.bloomberg. com/news/articles/2015-04-14/fossil-fuels-just-lost-the-race-against-renewables
22 Cameron A. Government U-turn on renewables shows gas, oil and nuclear are still favourites. The Guardian [Internet]. London and Manchester; 2015 Dec; Available from: http://www.theguardian.com/sustainable-business/2015/dec/ 20/government-u-turn-renewables-gas-oil-nuclear-favourites
23 DECC. Assessment SMRT. Early Market Engagement Announcement. 2015;(March).
24 Milmo D, Harvey F. Nuclear giants RWE and E.ON drop plans to build new UK reactors. The Guardian Online [Internet]. London and Manchester; 2012; Available from: http://www.theguardian.com/environment/2012/mar/29/nuclear-reactors-rwe-eon-energy
25 Wynn Kirby P. Europe's new nuclear experience casts a shadow over Hinkley. The Guardian Online [Internet]. London and Manchester; 2014 Mar; Available from: http://www.theguardian.com/environment/2014/mar/25/europes-new-nuclear-experience-casts-a-shadow-over-hinkley
26 Gosden E. Hinkley Point C: the story so far. The Daily Telegraph [Internet]. London; 2015 Mar; Available from: http://www.telegraph.co.uk/

news/earth/energy/nuclearpower/11404344/Hinkley-Point-new-nuclear-power-plant-the-story-so-far.html
27 Broomby R. Questions about UK scrutiny of Chinese nuclear tie-up [Internet]. BBC News Online. 2015 [cited 2015 Jan 15]. Available from: http://www.bbc.co.uk/news/uk-politics-30778427
28 Samuel H. New UK nuclear plants under threat as 'serious anomaly' with model found in France. The Daily Telegraph [Internet]. London; 2015 Apr; Available from: http://www.telegraph.co.uk/news/worldnews/europe/france/11546271/New-UK-nuclear-plants-under-threat-as-serious-anomaly-with-model-found-in-France.html
29 Macalister T. EDF Finance Minister resigns. The Guardian Online [Internet]. London and Manchester; 2016 Mar; Available from: http://www.theguardian.com/environment/2016/mar/07/hinkley-point-c-nuclear-project-in-crisis-as-edf-finance-director-resigns
30 The Week. Hinkley Point nuclear project could still be postponed. The Week Magazine Online [Internet]. 2016; Available from: http://www.theweek.co.uk/60778/hinkley-point-nuclear-project-could-still-be-postponed
31 DECC. DECC Contracts for Difference auction [Internet]. London; 2016. Available from: https://www.gov.uk/government/uploads/system/uploads/attachment_data/file/407059/Contracts_for_Difference_-_Auction_Results_-_Official_Statistics.pdf
32 The UK Govenment's Taskforce on Sustainable Consumption. Decentralised Energy: Business Opportunity in Resource Efficiency and Carbon Management [Internet]. Cambridge: University of Cambridge; 2008. Available from: http://www.cisl.cam.ac.uk/publications/publication-pdfs/decentralised-energy.pdf
33 Brown P. Voodoo Economics and the doomed nuclear renaissance. London; 2008.
34 Birmingham Policy Comission. The Future of Nuclear Technology in the UK. Birmingham; 2012.
35 Environmental Audit Committee. Keeping the lights on: Nuclear, Renewables and Climate Change. Vol. I. London; 2006.
36 Political Resources. UK political party manifestos [Internet]. Political Resources webpages. 1997. Available from: http://www.politicsresources.net/area/uk/man/man97.htm
37 PIU. The Energy Review [Internet]. London; 2002. Available from: http://www.gci.org.uk/Documents/TheEnergyReview.pdf
38 DTI. Our Energy Future: Creating a Low Carbon Economy. London; 2003.
39 Taylor S. The fall and rise of nuclear power in Britain. Cambridge: UIT Cambridge; 2016.
40 Royal Courts of Justice. The Queen on the applications of Greenpeace limited Vs Secretary of State for Trade and Industry' [Internet]. London; 2007. Available from: http://www.greenpeace.org.uk/MultimediaFiles/
41 House of Commons Trade and Industry Select Committee. New nuclear?

Examining the issues. London: The Stationary Office; 2006.
42 BBC News. Blair defiant over nuclear plans [Internet]. BBC News Online. 2007 [cited 2007 Jan 12]. Available from: http://news.bbc.co.uk/1/hi/uk_politics/6366725.stm
43 Vidal J. New nuclear row as green groups pull out. The Guardian Online [Internet]. London and Manchester; 2007 Sep; Available from: http://www.theguardian.com/environment/2007/sep/07/nuclearindustry.nuclear power
44 BERR. A White Paper on Nuclear Power, Meeting the energy challenge. London; 2008.
45 KOFAC. About Us [Internet]. Naval Ship Building North West Webpages. 2016 [cited 2016 Apr 15]. Available from: http://www.navalshipbuilding.co.uk/navalship_home.asp?ID=HOMA
46 Schank JF, Riposo J, Birkler J, Chiesa J. THe United Kingdom's Submarine Industrial Base Volume 1: Sustaining Design and Production Resources. Pittsburgh: RAND Corporation; 2005.
47 Schank JF, Cook CR, Murphy R, Chiesa J, Pung H, Birkler J. The United Kingdom's Nuclear Submarine Industrial Base Volume 2: Ministry of Defence Roles and Required Technical Resources. Arlington: RAND Corporation; 2005.
48 Raman R, Murphy R, Smallman L, Schank JF, Birkler J, Chiesa J. The United Kingdom's Nuclear Submarine Industrial Base Volume 3: Options for Initial Fuelling. Arlington: RAND Corporation; 2005.
49 Ministry Of Defence. Defence Industrial Strategy: Defence White Paper [Internet]. London: The Stationary Office; 2005. 286-310 p. Available from: http://www.informaworld.com/openurl?genre=article&doi=10.1080/14702430802252545&magic=crossref
50 Stocker J. The United Kingdom and Nuclear Deterrence. Oxon: Routledge; 2007.
51 Ireland G. Beyond Artful : Government and Industry Roles in Britain's Future Submarine Design , Build and Support. The Royal United Services Institute Whitehall Report 3-07. London: Royal United Services Institute; 2007.
52 Cogent. Power People: The Civil Nuclear Workforce 2009-2025. Warrington; 2009.
53 Ministry Of Defence. The United Kingdom's Future Detterent Capability. London: The Stationary Office; 2008.
54 The Nuclear Institute. Nuclear Institute [Internet]. Nuclear Institute Web pages. 2016 [cited 2016 Apr 12]. Available from: http://www.nuclearinst.com/ Homepage
55 Oxford Economics. The economic benefit of improving the UK's nuclear supply chain capabilities. Oxford: Oxford Economics Institute; 2013. 1-122

Reviews

Leen Words

Neil Fulwood & David Sillitoe (Eds.), *More Raw Material: Work inspired by Alan Sillitoe*, Lucifer Press, 2015, 240 pages, paperback ISBN 9780993424106, £9.00

Inspired by its honorand's own interwoven fiction and familial reminiscences, *Raw Material* (1972), this multi-authored anthology of prose and verse is a splendid tribute to Nottingham's best known (but not only) author. Immediate applause, too, for the physical pleasure afforded by the luxurious, indeed sensuous, paper on which it is printed. I doubt this Nottingham-based press is flush with money, but it has certainly pulled out all the stops here, a rebuking contrast to the many shoddy productions from other quarters. Readers may amplify their pleasure by the YouTube preservation of the book's unveiling at the Nottingham Poetry Festival event in Five Leaves Bookshop. YouTube also has various other Sillitoeana, most delightfully Alan Needham's crawl through twenty-one Nottingham pubs.

Since many remember Sillitoe mainly or exclusively (the film versions helped) through his first two novels – you all know which ones – this comports an important reminder that he regarded himself mainly as a poet, a genre as prominent as his novels and other ventures. Palpable influences here of his mentor, famous Classicist-novelist-poet Robert Graves (an early mentor, who – a somewhat premature act of friendship – in 1965 proposed Sillitoe for the Nobel Prize) and his wife, American poet Ruth Fainlight. Speaking of the latter, unless it was her choice, I would have expected a greater presence here. She is, after all, as eminent in her chosen fields as her husband. But all we get of her is a single-page Preface, a couple of black-and-white snaps, and a single poem, 'The Motorway', adumbrating their joint travels.

By the way, I mentioned Graves' classicism because, whilst in hospital for his tuberculosis, Sillitoe devoted much time to reading Greek and Latin literature in translation – a side of Arthur Seaton's creator not always remembered.

Although not a natural-born Nottinghamian (I'm a Lincolnshire 'Yellowbelly'), Sillitoe's Nottingham is partly mine also. I lived there 1956-62, as undergraduate, graduate, and commuting History lecturer to Loughborough College, before fleeing to Australia. Apart from digs in

Beeston, Chilwell, and West Bridgford, plus a brief 'crash' at Pat Jordan's 4 Dane Street bookshop, I actually lodged in Sillitoe's Radford whilst toiling not at Raleigh but the other (then) industrial giant, Player's. I can't claim to have been a friend of Sillitoe, but met him in group conversations both at university Socialist Society meetings and on the occasional 'demo'.

Fifty-something contributors comprise this memorial volume, which provides their capsule biographical and bibliographical details, these serving also in lieu of an index. Several naturally recall Sillitoe at personal levels well beyond my own. There is a good deal of poetry, the merits and demerits of each individual piece being beyond my allotted space and competence to dissect. As to the prose entries, largely and rightly in the Sillitoe manner, I am frankly not always sure if we are to take some of them as factual or fictional.

In terms of enjoyment, this need not too much matter. It certainly did not affect my particular pleasure in John King's 'See No Evil' and Mel Fisher's 'My Mate Sid'. An unequivocal and poignant essay is Tony Roe's 'From Gosling, R'. Gosling evoked Nottingham in his memoir *Personal Copy*, mentioning inter alios local CPGB stalwart John Peck, whom I remember seeing in 1956 being knocked from his Slab Square soapbox by John Daniels (senior) as he was parroting the *Daily Worker* line on Hungary

Ross Bradshaw's 'The Nottingham Issue' is a key element, emphasising as it does that Sillitoe was not some extraordinary local 'One-Off', but part of a rich Nottingham tradition of working-class literature. Individuals mentioned include Philip Callow (*The Hosanna Man*, 1956) and Michael Standen (*Start Somewhere*, 1965) on the male side, with a sideways glance at middle-class, Booker Prize-winning novelist Stanley Middleton's rare excursion into working-class life and culture in *Harris's Requiem* (1960), and passing mentions of the Broxtowe Estate's Derrick Buttress (featured elsewhere in the collection) and ephemeral teenage prodigy Pat McGrath (*The Green Leaves of Nottingham*, 1970 – Bradshaw could find no further trace of him, nor could my Google finger).

On the female side, Bradshaw adduces Ruth Adam (no titles cited), Hilda Lewis (*Penny Lace*, 1942), Jenny McLeod (*Stuck up a Tree*, 1998, set in black St Ann's), and Nicola Monaghan (*The Killing Jar*, 2007, another Broxtowe Estate setting, owing much to Sillitoe's personal encouragement).

Unlike Samuel Johnson on Milton's 'Paradise Lost', I could have wished this essay longer. No mention of the famous B.S. Johnson's 'experimental' *The Unfortunates* (1969, its settings, notably Forest's City

Ground, obviously Nottingham). As Sillitoe, Derrick Buttress moves successfully between memoirs, plays, and poetry. Same goes for Callow and Standen, both far more prolific and applauded than Bradshaw discloses. Jenny Mcleod's plays are singled out in Keith Peacock's *Thatcher's Theatre* (1999), whilst Nicola Monaghan's *The Killing Jar* was described in Hephzibah Anderson's *Guardian* review (available online) as 'a brew of hyperbolic nastiness, pilled up with flat-vowelled literary flourishes ... The rhythm of her language yields its own momentum.'

I least liked Bruce Wilson's mean-spirited attack on Karel Reisz' film of *Saturday Night and Sunday Morning*. Of course, *de gustibus non est disputandum* and all that, but I thought Albert Finney ideal as Arthur, and what red-blooded man could not have drooled over the beauty of Shirley Anne Field? Wilson's onslaught on Brenda's abortion is misleading. The gin-hot bath routine is not 'shrugged off', but (unlike the novel) simply fails. Censorship may have played a part here, likewise in reducing Arthur's spewing over a couple to spilling his beer over them.

My Nottingham Classics Professor, Edward Thompson (then involved – as I – with Gerry Healy's Trotskyite circus) remarked to me how astonished he was by the violence in the book. I attended the film's Nottingham premiere, now recalling with amusement the shocked gasps from some ladies at Arthur's using the word 'bloody' – *autres temps autres moeurs* indeed.

The penultimate photograph is of Sillitoe's grave in Highgate Cemetery, suitably sharing space with Karl Marx. A copy of this superlative commemoration should be placed thereon amidst the usual floral tributes.

Barry Baldwin
www.luciferpress.co.uk *Calgary, Canada*

Russian Interest

Donald Rayfield, Jeremy Hicks, Olga Makarova (editors), *The Garnett Book of Russian Verse: A Treasury of Russian Poets from 1730 to 1996 (Russian and English Edition)*, Garnett Press, 2013, 688 pages, ISBN 9780956468321, £25

This beautiful book, the second edition of the original 2000 publication, aims 'to make accessible to the interested reader a body of poetry as significant as anything the human spirit has produced'. Its intended readership ranges from 'those with a rudimentary knowledge but strong interest in Russian, to university students of Russian literature.' The latter group will have access to seventy-five poets with useful and discreet cribs on each page. They may be directed to it by tutors and reading lists.

What I find more interesting and exciting is the idea of it being a 'bedside book for a reader of poetry'. I'm guessing that a proficient reader of Russian might enjoy dipping into its wealth and finding something new every time, but it is also a superb introduction.

The cover is striking, the font clear and the English prose crib unassuming, an aid to unlocking the text rather, the editors claim, than 'a text with equal rights to the reader's mind'. That from the introduction which, of course, I did not read before engaging with the poems themselves, but which proved interesting and useful as a history of Russian poetry and its connection with other literatures.

Perhaps I should say at this point that I belong to the group of 'those with a rudimentary knowledge but strong interest in Russian'. I have started to study it at a time of my life when memorising vocabulary has become harder and the chance of a prolonged immersion in the language is receding rapidly, so I found, as I sat by a fire with the book on my lap, that I was coming to the book as above all else a reader of poetry. I did what I always do with an anthology. I read randomly, albeit slowly, relying heavily on the literal translation, struggling with pronunciation but gradually relaxing into reading whatever caught my eye, the name of a familiar poet, an easily accessible first line. ('I don't know ...' (Osip Mandelshtam), 'She loves me? She loves me not?' (Mayakovsky). And anything short.

At this point I felt justified in buying a new and larger dictionary, but it was also at this point that I was able to let go, to read a chosen poem, over and over, sometimes glancing at the translation, but also letting myself become familiar with the structure, the rhymes, the word order and, above all, the rhythm. What matters about getting to grips with a poem, I realised, was not so different from reading in your native language. Which brings me to, perhaps, the most helpful thing about the prose translations at the bottom of the page. They are not intrusive or prescriptive. They reminded me of watching a foreign film with subtitles when you become so engrossed in taking in what's going on that you feel you are understanding the language as clearly as if you could hear it.

I found some days that one poem was enough. I could tell which parts of speech most words were, but once a poem had caught my attention for long enough I found myself looking up most of the words I didn't already know. Slow, but kind of mindful. Pointless, one might say, given my impaired memorising skills, but so rewarding when returning after a night's sleep I found myself, rudimentary knowledge and all, simply reading the text, getting it, letting the whole poem work on me.

Marina Tsvetaeva, one of the poets I was already familiar with through the beautiful versions of Elaine Feinstein, is well represented. I loved 'Two Trees'. Mysterious, but graspable with the help of a translation that doesn't pretend to be other than literal, and Mikhail Lermontov's 'Last Testament' absorbed me for the whole of a journey across Ireland. I'm looking forward, now, to enjoying Pushkin to whom forty-four pages are devoted.

When I first engaged with this book I felt that I would have liked more information about individual poets. Certainly not in the text itself, where you only want the poem, but in the appendix often found in anthologies. The editors explain that lack of space made that an impossible undertaking and refer the reader to encyclopaedias. Fair enough. Moreover, I decided as I spent more and more time just enjoying the experience, one of the joys of engaging in a foreign language and literature is that you owe nothing to the canon, that you find what appeals to you and only then try to put it into context. I'm looking forward to that too. The student of Russian literature to whom I don't seem to have paid much attention might not need this book to be as beautiful to look at, as enticing, as I did. For the reader of poetry, however limited their language proficiency, it is sheer delight.

Sheelagh Gallagher

Disaster Tour

Antony Loewenstein, *Disaster Capitalism: Making a Killing out of Catastrophe*, Verso, 376 pages, hardback ISBN 9781784781156, £16.99, ebook ISBN 9781784781163, £16.99

This is a hard-hitting attack on the predatory activities of big business, ever ready to cash in on a catastrophe, whether it is privatising violence in Afghanistan or evicting indigenous people from areas 'needed' for mineral extraction. The rapacious activities of the likes of Serco, Rio Tinto, Halliburton and G4S have been investigated and exposed by the intrepid and independent Australian journalist, Antony Loewenstein. Following the ideas of an earlier work by Naomi Klein, *The Shock Doctrine*, it gives extensive detail of the global phenomenon whereby the policies of Western companies and politicians take advantage of both natural and unnatural catastrophes.

The first chapter takes us to Afghanistan and Pakistan, into the ugly world of the privatised military (mercenaries), who regard killing and torture as all in a day's work. There the US government, aware of the unpopularity of foreign wars, has devolved to private suppliers many of the tasks previously undertaken by the armed services. These contracts are handed to the large corporations who, in turn, sub-contract out the more frontline duties to the likes of the notorious Blackwater. All this is set against a background of abject poverty, chronic drug addiction, war with the Taliban, and grasping corruption at even the highest levels of the Afghan state. The activities of these giant corporations are carried out on a global basis and Loewenstein has necessarily pursued them in many countries.

Loewenstein spent time in Greece, mainly prior to Syriza forming a government, but even then Greece had the dual problems of imposed austerity together with a steady flow of migrants. The author observes the ordinary people of Greece struggling against the dire programme of austerity imposed by the Troika, and the violent victimisation of migrants by the police and the fascist Golden Dawn. *Disaster Capitalism* certainly sets the scene for what has followed, with wholesale privatisation of previously nationalised companies and the intensification of austerity.

In Haiti, Loewenstein is shocked to discover that much of the damage from the earthquake, which struck some five years ago in Port-au-Prince, still exists, whilst Haitians try to eke out a living among the rubble, garbage and sewage-strewn streets. How a country with so much potential could end up in this terrible state is explained. The political corruption, the non-governmental organisations (NGOs) with their 'one-model-fits-all mindset', the interference of foreign states (particularly the United States) in the political life of the country, the squandering of aid, and the failure to release monies to local indigenous civil institutions have all played their part. Finally, to add to the mayhem, are the activities of the multinationals, many of which managed to obtain contracts by backdoor pressure in Washington. These foreign companies often gave poor performance for the Haitians but, of course, made large profits for themselves.

In Papua New Guinea (PNG) it was the same old story of an over-eager government wanting to take a development path that would benefit the few at the expense of the many. The former colonial power, Australia, and a multinational corporation, Rio Tinto, want to control the mineral resources of the massive Panguna mine at Bougainville. The mining had already led to armed conflict from 1989 to 1997, which effectively closed the mine. Now there are plans to reopen it when it has already caused an environmental disaster with toxic waste containing asbestos and heavy metals, and has ruined much agricultural land with the mine spoil.

The final three chapters illustrate the influence and power of the multinational companies in the developed countries of Australia, the United States and here in the United Kingdom. In the UK, Loewenstein records the largely privatised housing of asylum seekers – a system which has been contracted out by the Home Office to private companies, resulting in often sub-standard housing. Once given refugee status, the people concerned are moved out of the initial dwelling and become the responsibility of inadequately funded charities and the benefits system, often meaning a further deterioration in housing and living arrangements. However, things are a lot bleaker in Campsfield and Yarl's Wood detention centres run by Mitie and Serco, as *Disaster Capitalism* makes clear. The inherently cruel way migrants are treated is exemplified by the killing of Jimmy Mubenga, whilst forcibly restrained as he was being deported to Angola after living in the UK for 14 years with his wife and five children.

In his native Australia the author visits the refugee detention centre on Christmas Island and gathers information on what is actually happening there, and on other islands in the region where refugees are kept. This was despite the efforts of Serco, and the Australian Department of Immigration and Border Protection (DIBP), who indulged in much subterfuge to prevent him interviewing the incarcerated. The ruse of isolating refugees on distant islands away from the mainland was dreamt up by the conservative government of John Howard, who in 2001 directed 438 refugees on board a Norwegian ship to the island of Nauru. This marks yet another chapter in Australia's brutal treatment of any race that is not European in origin.

The section on the United States deals with the companies who make a profit out of the vast prison system. In 1980 the prison population was about 300,000: it is now more than two million, similar in size to Stalin's Gulag at its high point in 1953. The incarcerated are overwhelmingly Latino or black and this leads one to believe that such numbers must be the result of institutional racism, to which the recent police shootings of unarmed people of colour will attest. The author visits prisons, fraternises with prison personnel employed by the private companies, and notes the police with their body armour and latest crowd control equipment, comparable to that of US soldiers in Iraq. Of course, there is a lot of money in the correctional industry, but it goes to the corporate rich; wages for the operatives are usually low, and this applies to many of the areas investigated by the author.

Loewenstein presumably sees 'Disaster Capitalism' as a new predatory form of capitalism that has taken root since the demise of the Soviet bloc. What cannot be ignored is the brazen self-confidence that the neo-liberal philosophy and the capitalist restoration in Eastern Europe and China bestowed upon our elite. Although the financial crash of 2008 did temporarily deflate the hubris of our leaders, things have continued in very much the same pattern since, and the gap between the 1% and the rest of us continues to grow.

Whether or not there is another economic type called 'Disaster Capitalism' I am not sure. I suspect that the mechanisms of capitalism have often been lubricated by unfortunate occurrences. In this context we should not forget capitalism's undeniable ability to engender the most cataclysmic of events in the 20th century in the form of two world wars. Loewenstein, however, whatever kind of capitalism he calls it, has done an admirable job demonstrating its exploitative and de-humanising effects both in the developing and the developed world. It is a powerful indictment of the predatory nature of multinational companies and their ability to suborn national governments. Also he has shown admirable courage in investigating and writing about areas where violence has been simmering for some time and his book deserves to be widely read. It is packed with information to counter the more supine media analysis of globalisation and its 'free' markets that we are routinely bombarded with. *Disaster Capitalism* is full of anecdotal insights and interviews and deserves to be read by everyone who is struggling to bring about a new world order of peace and equality.

John Daniels

Stale Bread

Jeremy Seabrook, *Pauperland: Poverty and the Poor in Britain*, C. Hurst and Co, 2015, 288 pages, paperback ISBN 9781849045841, £9.99

With a title *Pauperland* and a front cover illustrating thin-sliced, white bread, this book was always going to be difficult. First published in 2013, Jeremy Seabrook's exploration of why poverty persists in Britain in the midst of great wealth is now available in paperback. The hardback has been lauded by *The Times*, *The Sunday Times* and *The Guardian* amongst others. Their praiseworthy comments appear on the paperback's back cover. Seabrook may be known to *Spokesman* readers for his journalistic forays into a range of social issues over the last fifty years, but what might he be able to say about the history of the poor, and poverty more generally, in Britain?

Seabrook is neither a historian nor a social scientist. In fact, he has little time for the latter or for the 'numberless functionaries' whose work involves contact with today's poor. So his purpose in writing this book is not to present carefully-sourced, historical or social analysis and discussion but, instead, to pose a series of questions to which his answers are simply 'tentative and provisional'. The questions range over ideas about the nature of poverty and how they have changed over time, from rural to industrial to post-industrial Britain. 'Far from the least' of his enquiries is '... where do the attitudes which animate popular resentment of the poor come from?' The questions seem straightforward enough although they are not dealt with straightforwardly by the author because he has deeper concerns about what he calls 'sufficiency'. Indeed, the idea of 'sufficiency' underlies and animates the different chapters and gives Seabrook the opportunity to introduce 'wealth' to the discussion. Unfortunately, it also gives him the opportunity to be selective and judgemental to an extraordinary degree.

The first half of *Pauperland* explores how the poor law developed from Elizabethan times through to the 1834 Poor Law and beyond and highlights how attitudes towards poverty and the poor changed over that time. Using contemporaneous writers, philosophers, parliamentary reports and personal accounts Seabrook creates four, long, discursive chapters on the rural poor which mix historical fact, other writers' views and his own concerns. These sequences are not always easy to follow, although there are some eye-popping views here including commentary on the way the poor law worked in the decades of agricultural depression in the early part of the nineteenth century. For example, writing in 1786, the Reverend Joseph Townsend, vicar of Pewsey in Wiltshire (one of the poorest parts of England) believed that hunger brought the rural poor into line and reinforced proper deference. He bemoaned the poor law as 'more than liberal' since '... what cause have they [the poor] to fear when they are assured, that if by their indolence and extravagance, by their drunkenness and vices, they should be reduced to want, they shall be abundantly supplied, not only with food and raiment but with their accustomed luxuries at the expence (sic) of others'. As Seabrook points out, Townsend contributed to the hardening of attitudes among those of his class at that time and later. These comments appear in a section devoted to a discussion of the Speenhamland system of poor law, the Swing riots in 1830-2, and the more restrictive poor laws introduced following an investigatory Commission and legislation in 1834.

A number of points may be made here about Seabrook's writing which also apply more generally to the rest of the book. Firstly, Seabrook's historical analysis is less than careful, especially in explanations of change. For example, contrary to what he says, most landowners at this time did not prefer more generous poor law provision (the Speenhamland system) to stave off civil unrest and neither did the amount paid out nationally to 'paupers' increase in the first part of the nineteenth century. It fell dramatically, even though the numbers needing poor relief who were unemployed or underemployed increased as farmers continued to reduce wages, especially through the use of threshing machinery and the introduction of different work patterns (day labouring instead of annual hiring or boarding). It is these features that precipitated riots, rick-burning and machine breaking across the agricultural south and east of England in 1830-2 and which, for a time at least, delayed the imposition of a more restrictive regime of poor law. A more detailed historical analysis may be found in Hobsbawn and Rude's book *Captain Swing*.

Seabrook's writing style is often overly complicated, value-laden and unclear. For example, he tells us that:

> 'Burke's animadversions on the Speenhamland system were vindicated. While the "right to life" is a noble principle (echoed over time by the Green and socialist movements) in practice, it meant that farmers were not required to pay a living wage, since the parish would make up the difference.'

Linked to this, the emphasis on answering, however tentatively, a range of broad questions leads him to rely on specific writers and reports which seemingly encapsulate ideas about poverty. He draws a great deal here on Townsend, Burke, the *Report of the Poor Law Commission,* and writings by Jeremy Bentham and Thomas Malthus. A good editor would have chopped a lot. For example, do we need:

> 'Bentham starkly enunciates the value-system of the self-regulating market, to which he ascribes miraculous powers, since through its workings, human nature, with all its vicious propensities, would emerge, cleansed and capable of social good. Capitalism was to become redemptive: in its baptism of the people by total immersion, it scooped up and absorbed some of the beliefs of Christianity. Similar patterns of feeling would later nourish Marx, whose transforming doctrines also focussed on a form of redemption, albeit secular.' (p81)

From the overly long to the exceedingly short: chapter 5, 'Voices of the poor', is three pages, made up of personal accounts of five agricultural labourers (the oldest born in 1804, the youngest born in 1844) from different parts of England. These were collected by Jane Cobden Unwin who published them, in 1904, under the title *The hungry forties*. Unsurprisingly given her background, this was a book published in support of free trade (although Seabrook does not tell us that). He tells us that these 'voices' are an 'authentic account of the life of farm labourers in the first half of the nineteenth century'. A social scientist would have made something of these, placing them in context and highlighting particular features, especially incomes and food, but no attempt has been made to do that. This is a great pity as there is much that could be said. Seventy years after Pewsey's Reverend Townsend's complaints about farm labourers' extravagance, the economic situation had not improved. By 1850, Wiltshire, a predominantly rural county, had the highest percentage of paupers to total population at 16.1% despite the 1834 poor law and the deterrent nastiness of the workhouse

Social historian John Burnett pointed out that 'The general state of the rural labourer between 1850-1914 was one of chronic poverty and want, acute in the 1850s, slightly better towards the end' (p.133). He refers to a survey undertaken in 1863 where the nature of meals consumed by agricultural labourers' families across the country was detailed (Burnett, 1989, pp.141-5). Most poor, rural families lived in cottages or huts that had no oven or range and the bulk of food was boiled in a large iron pot over an open fire or fried. A fire would not be lit all the time as many could not afford fuel. In Wiltshire, the normal fare for a family in 1863 was:

> Breakfast: water broth, bread and butter;
> Dinner: the husband and children have bacon (sometimes), cabbage, bread and butter; the wife had tea;
> Supper: potatoes or rice.

Unsurprisingly, a rural exodus during the last thirty years of the nineteenth century saw 100,000 agricultural labourers each decade leaving the land for work in towns and cities, the United States or British colonies. Unfortunately, Seabrook chooses to end this part of the book and this chapter by remarking that the accounts of these agricultural workers were 'coloured by an intense feeling of injustice, and they are not less tendentious than the evidence given by informants to the Commission on the Poor Law'. This is not an appropriate remark to make of people who would often have been living on the edge of starvation and whose lives we can barely imagine. Chapter 6, 'The industrial poor', begins:

> 'By 1834, the ideology governing attitudes towards the poor was settled; and everything that occurred subsequently was a working out of the conflict between doctrines of the free market and the need to temper its most baleful effects by legislation. The context in which this took place was determined, first of all, by a recognition that the best protection for the working (and non-working) poor lay in collective action and organisation. Confronted by the growing assertiveness of the labour movement, governments responded with increasing solicitude, passing laws ... as well as providing public amenities ...' (p.111)

This essentially Whiggish or liberal account, taking no account of class antagonism or struggle, is not followed by a detailed account of how this apparent change of heart occurred and its ameliorative effects on the poor. Instead, Seabrook relies again for his source material on writers' attitudes towards the working class. His antagonism towards Marxism or socialism is revealed here, too, in that the most obvious and influential text from the period (Engels' *Condition of the Working Class in England*) with its descriptions of the poor of Manchester in the 1840s (whose horrendous living conditions were replicated in Leeds, Sheffield, Birmingham and London) was simply referred to in passing as Engels' 'lurid vision of the fate of the working-class'. Astonishingly, Engels and Manchester are not mentioned again while an unknown writer on conditions in Merthyr Tydfil in 1848 is quoted in full.

Seabrook discusses the impact of industrial life on people and communities in the next two chapters. He uses a large number of individual personal histories to illustrate points: from Rowntree's work in London or Booth's researches in York in the early 1900s or his own work, in Lancashire mill towns, in the 1960s. Some accounts are dry and factual, drawn from investigators' notebooks, but Seabrook's are full of dialogue and detail, either real or conjured up in his imagination to recall past times. These accounts provide powerful testimonies of the difficult struggles to survive that many poor people endured up to the 1970s, even with the safety net of the welfare state. But again the writing meanders and is imbued with anger and a strong moral sensibility (which may be acceptable to some but is irritating to others). This is no more so than in his descriptions of the impact of poverty on the industrial poor and the establishment of the welfare state in 1945:

> 'If conditions were degrading and people perished, poverty also called forth resistance and dignity, mutuality and self-sacrifice, a sensibility reminiscent, if of anything, of the elective holy poverty of the early saints ...' (p.147)

And so it goes on. By Chapter 9, Seabrook has moved on to discuss 'modernised poverty'. 'Primitive poverty' as he calls it 'exposed most of humankind to hunger, pestilence and the arbitrary rule of the powerful'. Modernised poverty, by contrast, is 'non-participation ... a punitive exclusion that condemned the poor to wander like souls permanently exiled from Elysium, the inhabitants of a limbo ...' And it gets worse. The poor today live in

> 'slum estates ... where mainly the defeated, the wretched and the demoralised ... remain. Although it requires costly administration to keep them where they belong, no overseers, parish officials or beadles are required to judge whether this is an appropriate place for them, or to bear the costs of despatching them there ... To these, the captive poor, has been entrusted the task of demonstrating the continuing penury of wealthy societies: they are the living embodiment of the need for more economic growth, fed by the strident neediness of their assertive hungers.' (p.155)

These 'orphans of the market' ... 'are doomed to play out lives of self-harm, destructiveness, wrecking and robbing their own community, stealing from "their own kind", dealing in forbidden substances, cheating and cozening, an illegal mimicry of approved entrepreneurial activity.' (p.156)

This is a world away from research findings by social scientists including recent research on St Ann's in Nottingham (see my review of Lisa McKenzie's *Getting By* in *Spokesman 129*) and it beggars belief that he follows this with accounts of individuals and families he has met to show how the 'neglected interiors of the houses reflect the ragged psychic interiors' of the 'deprived'. Do the people he interviews or meets never see what he writes about them? It is Seabrook's contention that consumerism has destroyed any independent culture that the working class ever had. By contrast:

> '... the slum dwellers of Asia and Africa have memories of self-provisioning – capacity to build a shelter, a remembrance of famine foods and of herbs and plants with healing or nutritious properties ... All such knowledge has been erased from the mental storehouse of the poor in "advanced" societies ... If people live off the dregs of the consumer market, this is because they are the dregs of a labour market ...' (p.157)

'The impoverishment of riches' is the last chapter and it contains Seabrook's view of what needs to change. In his view, the position of the poor will never be helped by 'the legions of poverty-abaters'. Instead, definitions of poverty linked to monetary wealth (citing ideas such as Peter

Townsend's relative poverty) should be abandoned. After all, he argues, they are only 'a re-hash of the work of older cartographers of Maps of Pauperland' and 'to abandon redistribution is to acknowledge that the have-nots merit the nothing they possess'. (p.225) Attitudes towards the wealthy also need to change to enable the growth of different values including that simple 'sufficiency' is enough instead of the constant striving after commodities and monetary riches which is consumerism. As with preceding chapters, Seabrook uses other writers to bolster these ideas, but what is notable about this one is that the kernel of these ideas is almost hidden in the overblown metaphorical and religious language and long commentary attacking those he believes have led society in the wrong direction – namely, socialists, the Labour Party, 'poverty-abaters', social scientists, the wealthy, philanthropists and 'goodwill ambassadors'. It is very difficult indeed to get to the end of all this without feeling that the author is flailing around, angry at the world which has been taking little notice for the last fifty years. But this is not a surprise. The language and ideas are largely inaccessible. His views about political and social change seem simplistic. His vision of the future is scarcely realistic. Pauperland and sliced white bread? Thanks - but no thanks.

Cathy Davis

References

John Burnett. (1989, 3rd edition) *Plenty and want: a social history of food in England from 1815 to the present day*. London: Routledge

E.J. Hobsbawm and George Rude. (1969) *Captain Swing*. London: Lawrence and Wishart

Eight Conflicts

Patrick Cockburn, *Chaos and Caliphate: The Jihadi Struggle for the Middle East*, OR Books, New York and London, 2016, 428 pages, paperback ISBN 9781682190289, £19, ebook ISBN 9781682190296, £10

Few journalists are as well informed on the Middle East and Central Asia, their history and current problems, as Patrick Cockburn. Since 2001 – sometimes at great personal risk – he has reported on the various wars in the region and he has now published, in *Chaos and Caliphate*, a selection of his notes, diary entries and reports, plus his reflections and conclusions.

Cockburn points out that there are now eight conflicts being fought in the region: in Afghanistan, Iraq, Libya, Syria, the Yemen, as well as

Somalia, north-east Nigeria, and between Kurds and Turks in Turkey. In the first four of these, military intervention principally by the West and, in the Yemen, principally by Saudi Arabia, has played a key role.

What comes out very clearly from his study is that the policies pursued by the West – even from its own narrow point of view – have largely failed and have compounded problems rather than resolved them.

Cockburn expected the West to encounter insuperable difficulties in Afghanistan. The Taliban were defeated by western military intervention in 2001 but made a comeback subsequently, primarily because of gross errors by the Afghan government of Hamid Karzai and its American backer. It was grossly corrupt. The Taliban retained considerable support within the Pashtun segment of the population (i.e. 42 per cent of the total) and it received the covert backing of Pakistan military intelligence. It remains a serious threat since the withdrawal of western military forces, and Osama bin Laden has achieved his aim of a continuing war between the western allies and the Muslim world.

In the case of Iraq, Cockburn expresses surprise that the US gave so little thought to the political consequences of its invasion. The Americans failed to recognise the divisions between Sunnis, Shias and Kurds. They failed to prevent widespread looting and, by dissolving the Iraqi army, they created a mass of near destitute soldiers. They also failed to realise that, once Saddam Hussein had been overthrown, the bulk of the Iraqi population wanted foreign troops to leave.

In 2006 Cockburn wrote

'It is seldom realised that the US and Britain have largely provoked the civil war that is raging across central Iraq.' [p.144]

Cockburn is critical of the application of the term 'Arab Spring' to developments in the Middle East and North Africa on the grounds that militant Islamism was an element in these rebellions that was overlooked.

In Libya, the uprising against Gaddafi was supported by Saudi Arabia and the Gulf monarchies – hardly bulwarks of democracy. NATO joined in and organised thousands of air strikes, without which Gaddafi would not have been overthrown. However, as Cockburn's reports at the time illustrate, David Cameron, British Foreign Secretaries William Hague and Philip Hammond, together with Hillary Clinton, badly misread the situation. The first measure enacted by the transitional government was to end the ban on polygamy. The US ambassador, Chris Stevens, was murdered, and Africans employed under the previous regime – particularly Christians – were persecuted and, in some cases, executed. Civil war followed. As Cockburn concluded: 'whatever the Western intentions, the result has been a disaster'. [p.242]

In Syria, the West, along with Saudi Arabia, the Gulf States and Turkey, wanted Bashar Assad to be overthrown and, when mass protests broke out against his rule in 2011, assumed that he would be. Saudi Arabia, Qatar and the West supplied the rebels with arms while Iran, Hezbollah and Russia supported Assad. According to Cockburn, 30 per cent of the population backed Assad, 30 per cent opposed him, and the remaining 40 per cent were not disposed to favour government or rebels.

Appalling as were all the Middle Eastern conflicts, in the Syrian civil war the results were worse, with hundreds of thousands of casualties and millions of refugees generated. In a mixed population comprising Sunnis, Shias, Alawites, Christians, Druze, Yazidis and Kurds, Cockburn identifies five different conflicts: a popular rising against Assad; Sunnis against Shias; Sunnis against Alawites; Iran against the US and Saudi Arabia; Russia against the West.

In the Yemen yet another bitter armed conflict is raging between Saudi Arabia and the Shi'ite Houthis who have driven out their President, Abed Mansour Hadi. Here, the US is supporting the fugitive President and Britain has supplied the Saudis with arms, while the Yemeni population is desperately short of food and water.

Across the region as a whole there is chaos, as indicated in the title of this book. However, there is also, as indicated in the title, the Caliphate. This is the regime otherwise known as ISIS (the Islamic State of Iraq and Syria), ISIL or Daesh, which is seeking to establish a caliphate under Abu Bakr al Baghdadi throughout the Middle East. It has already taken over much of Syria and northern Iraq and is a fanatical Sunni fundamentalist sect which is totally intolerant of all who do not accept it and comply with its tenets. It has its own versions of sharia law, and amputations, beheadings and floggings are regular punishments. Women are reduced to the status of chattels and are forced strictly to obey their husbands, even becoming suicide bombers. Shaving, western-style haircuts, art, music, philosophy, the teaching of evolution, etc., are forbidden. Christians, Shias, Alawites, Yazidis, dissident Sunnis in areas taken over have been killed or enslaved. The Islamic State is seeking to promote terrorism throughout the world to extend its rule.

Chaos and Caliphate is an encyclopaedic survey of events and hostilities in the Middle East and neighbouring areas over recent decades and has much to teach us. In the first place, it makes clear the idea that the US, Britain or any other powerful western country can create a western orientated democracy by military intervention is mistaken. It calls into question the close alliances forged with repressive governments – in particular those of the West with Saudi Arabia and the Gulf States. The efforts of Saudi Arabia to spread its Wahhabi faith is linked to jihadism. As is pointed out, 15 of the 19 hijackers on 9/11 were Saudis, like Osama bin Laden, and when he was killed by US forces, in 2011, Abu Bakr al Baghdadi pledged to launch 100 attacks in revenge for his death. The West averted its eyes when protests against the al Khalifa regime in Bahrain were brutally suppressed.

Patrick Cockburn has provided an invaluable account of the manner in which a quasi medieval reaction is sweeping across the Middle East and adjoining areas and the misguided policies of the West. His book should be read and studied by anyone seeking to understand events in the region and hopefully to campaign for more progressive policies.

Stan Newens

Letters on Albania

Blendi Fevziu (tr. Majlinda Nishku), *Enver Hoxha: The Iron Fist of Albania,* **I. B. Tauris, 2016, 312 pages, hardback ISBN 9781784534851, £25**

The Albanian original of this book appeared in 2011. Fevziu, ubiquitous journalist and TV presenter (see YouTube), graduated from Tirana University in 1991, hence must have been Party-approved. My Tirana contacts tell me he has a reputation among peers for cut-and-paste methods bordering on plagiarism.

Joanna Godfrey (I.B. Tauris editor) informs me this edition is not a straight translation but specially confected for English consumption by leading Albanologist Robert Elsie and Fevziu himself. Not quite sure where this leaves Majlinda Nishku, freelance translator formerly at Tirana University, a non-answerer of e-mails.

Chapter 17 is omitted, this lacuna absurdly requested by Fevziu as of no interest to English readers (Elsie). It would surely have fascinated them with its details of Enver impersonators along with dismissal of the widely-disbelieved story of kidnapped dentist Petar Shapallo, pedalled by Lloyd Jones' *Biografi* (1993); cf. my review, *Friends of Albania Newsletter* (Winter 1993). Various websites offer Carli Ruchala's similar tale featuring an equally suspect Ali Razhedi.

This English version adds a bibliography, an index (Enver himself missing!), and potted biographies of individual Albanians mentioned. But, apart from excluding occasional endnotes to chapters 1, 3, 5, 16 – why? – it also omits the facsimiles of Hoxha correspondence, and by reproducing only six of the original fifty-three photographs deprives readers of, for example, the macabre snap of Hoxha hand-in-hand with defence minister Beqir Balluku just three months before having him shot – pure *1984*.

Neither version mentions YouTube's innumerable Albanian TV items, from Hoxha's speeches and funeral to the 1983 trial of interior minister Kadri Hazbiu from the last great purge.

Elsie's Foreword claims this is 'the first serious book' on Hoxha. Odd, since he reviewed (*Südöst-Forschungen* 53, 1994, 544-546) Thomas Schreiber's *Enver Hodja: Le sultan rouge* (1994). Henry Çili's (Tirana European University) mentions Schreiber, also (getting both name and nationality wrong) Jon Halliday's *The Artful Albanian* (1986), not a biography proper but useful anthology of translated extracts from Hoxha's seventy-nine books with linking commentaries.

Fevziu (mentions Halliday, not Schreiber) unfairly ridicules these as 'mediocre and unrefined, lacking both expression and style'. Hoxha actually wrote with great humour and verve, by far the most readable of East European communist leaders. Also, the best read. Apart from his French teaching, Hoxha knew other languages, writes interestingly about ancient philosophy in *Two Friendly Peoples* (1985 – Albania and Greece), and in *With Stalin* (1978) discusses points of Homeric philology – surely a unique moment for inter-dictator colloquies.

However, Fevziu does demolish the allegation of James Pettier & Miranda Vickers (*Albania: From Anarchy to a Balkan Identity* (2000, p. 13) that Hoxha's later books were ghost-written, he being in dementia. Hoxha actually produced thirteen books during his last years, no signs of mental problems (physically, he suffered from diabetes and cardiac problems – here, one wonders about the role of tactfully-omitted ex-President Sali Berisha, Party-pampered heart specialist) until November 1984. I've seen the video of his Liberation Anniversary speech then – or was this one of those famous doubles?

As always, Hoxha is branded paranoid, both for his purges and those notorious concrete bunkers. Too simplistic. Although numerous individuals fell victim for such imaginary crimes as 'economic sabotage' or as 'enemies of The People', Hoxha was almost unseated to the point of public self-criticism (1947) by interior minister rival Koçi Xoxe, ironically preferred by Stalin as more proletarian than the dapper bourgeois Enver. Problem solved in 1949 when Xoxe was liquidated – allegedly strangled by 'The Butcher of Tirana', Mehmet Shehu.

Nor were fears of invasion unwarranted, given the failed (thanks to Philby's betrayal) Anglo-American assault (1949) and Soviet occupations of Hungary (1956) and Czechoslovakia (1968), especially after the rupture with Khrushchev over de-Stalinisation.

Hoxha executed uncountable thousands. Amnesty International calculated one-third of the population were in labour camps or internal exile. Fevziu provides an exhaustive chamber of horrors. No room, though, for the régime's achievements. As Stalin, Hoxha dragged his country from dark ages to modernity: elimination of illiteracy, countrywide electrification, the first railways – roads less vital, thanks to the ban on private vehicles, this giving Tirana a surrealist calm and an Eden for traffic policemen – the first university, rights for women. He also strove to create full employment (without taxes), maintain both national economic self-sufficiency and independence from power blocs.

Mixed results, but credit for trying, as with attempts to eradicate the age-old blood feuds in the northern mountains (cf. myself, *Chronicles*, January 1998, pp.16-18), now back in full swing.

All Hoxha assessments have two ineluctable topics: novelist Ismail Kadare's life and interior minister Mehmet Shehu's death.

Kadare gets the usual whitewash. I have frequently exposed this charlatan in *ReadySteady/Book* (UK), *I&NS* reviews, letters in *TLS*. Fevziu ignores Albanian newspaper publication (e.g. *Koha Jonë*, May 25, 1996) of Hoxha diary entries attesting their close friendship, Kadare's many privileges (passport, foreign travel, literary and political offices), also disclosures by ex-Sigurimi (Secret Police) Zylytftar Ramiz and other officers, plus Kapilani Resuli (Macedonian Truth Forum, on-line) that he was an informer (code-name 'General'). Genuine dissidents such as Kasëm Trebeshima and Mehmet Myftiu, punished for courageous public protests, were treated by Kadare with what even his admirer Elsie dubs 'extraordinary vindictiveness'. As for his well-publicized 'defection' to France (1990), sensing the Ramiz Alia régime was in collapse, ex-Romanian dissident blogger Renata Dumitrascu characterizes this as a good example of rat deserting sinking ship.

Tirana Radio (December 18, 1981) announced that Mehmet Shehu had committed suicide in a fit of nervous depression. Following year's newspapers said *u liquidua*. Thanks to Albanian syntactical nuances, this can mean 'killed himself' or 'was killed'. Fevziu (pp. 236, 244) is self-contradictory, as he is when describing Hoxha both as promiscuously gay (p.16) and energetic womanizer (p.31), or when giving Koçi Xoxe two separate birthplaces (pp. 117, 139). Western newspapers talked of 'shootouts' at dinner or at Central Committee meeting (I've heard the same from old Albanian acquaintances), ridiculed by Hoxha in his *Titoites* (1982) where Shehu is denounced (I've seen a cognate video) as a 'poly-agent' spying for half-a-dozen countries – you wonder how he kept his espionage diary straight.

In *Besa* 1 (1994, 19-27), I had a 'scoop' of sorts, publishing the only English translation of an interview published in the Italian Albanian language newspaper *Gazette Shqiptarë* (June 15 & 18, 1993) in which Shehu's chief bodyguard, Ali Çena, gives circumstantial evidence that Shehu was murdered by night at his villa.

None of this is in Fevziu. Nor does he include Jon Halliday's (*London Review of Books*, October 9, 1986) plausible claim – despite lively opposition in its Letters pages – that Party historian Arben Puto 'detonated lethal suspicion in a chronically suspicious mind' when he showed Hoxha some archival British documents naming Shehu as a potential agent.

The mystery remains. Shehu's son, novelist Baskim, inclines to suicide. Kadare leapt in with his (as with everything else) fictional *The Successor* (2011), pointing a finger at Hoxha's widow, Nexmije, as a kind of Borgia or Ptolemaic queen. (Fevziu's estimates of her actual influence wobble throughout.) One question should be obvious: if suicide, why all the frantic attempts to put him in the far-from-unique 'poli-agent' bracket? One answer: on Hoxha's own reckoning, every single interior minister from Xoxhe to Kadriu had been traitors, wryly adding they had been unmasked by The Party, all missed by the Sigurimi!.

Hoxha's sanguinary reign offers little humorous scope. For light relief, Fevziu might have mentioned Enver (youthful memories) consuming eight croissants for his first French breakfast, ironic for one who (diary entry) denounces Harry Pollitt's gluttony at a Moscow conference. Another irony not made clear for English readers is that 'Hoxha/Hodja' means 'priest', nor that his father was an imam, neither pedigree stopping him from proclaiming (1967) Albania the world's first officially atheist country.

On the credit side, Fevziu (p.216) is probably right to deny Hoxha poisoned intimate colleague Hysni Kapo (cp. Stalin and Kirov), and also provides (p.25) a tantalizing glimpse into Soviet infiltration of the Bloomsbury group (cf. Stephen Koch's books on this and its instigator, Willi Münzenberg), also (p.250) Hoxha's doctor Ulli Popa's theory (aired on Albanian TV) supporting Beria's supposed poisoning of Stalin.

Robert Elsie (e-mail) remarks, 'the original was very sloppy. But it is nevertheless a fascinating book' – I agree.

Barry Baldwin